SCOTTISH

Dane Love is the author of numerous books on Scotland in general and on Ayrshire in particular, where he lives with his wife and two children. He is descended from Robin Love, who fought for Bonnie Prince Charlie at the battles of Prestonpans and Culloden. He is the Honorary Secretary of the Scottish Covenanter Memorials Association and a Fellow of the Society of Antiquaries of Scotland. Dane Love is the author of *Scottish Covenanter Stories*, *The Man Who Sold Nelson's Column* – a collection of Scottish frauds and hoaxes, *Scottish Kirkyards*, *Jacobite Stories*, as well as various books on Ayrshire places and history.

www.dane-love.co.uk

By the same author:

Scottish Kirkyards
The History of Auchinleck – Village & Parish
Pictorial History of Cumnock
Pictorial History of Ayr
The Auld Inns of Scotland
Guide to Scottish Castles
Tales of the Clan Chiefs
Scottish Covenanter Stories
Ayr Stories
Ayrshire Coast
Scottish Spectres
Ayrshire: Discovering a County
Ayr Past and Present
Lost Ayrshire
The River Ayr Way
Ayr – the Way We Were
The Man Who Sold Nelson's Column
Jacobite Stories
The History of Sorn – Village & Parish
Legendary Ayrshire

SCOTTISH GHOSTS

DANE LOVE

AMBERLEY

First published 1995
This edition published 2009

Amberley Publishing
Cirencester Road, Chalford,
Stroud, Gloucestershire, GL6 8PE

www.amberley-books.com

British Library Cataloguing in Publication Data.
A catalogue record for this book is available from the British Library.

ISBN 978 1 84868 722 6

Typesetting and origination by Amberley Publishing
Printed in Great Britain

CONTENTS

MAPS

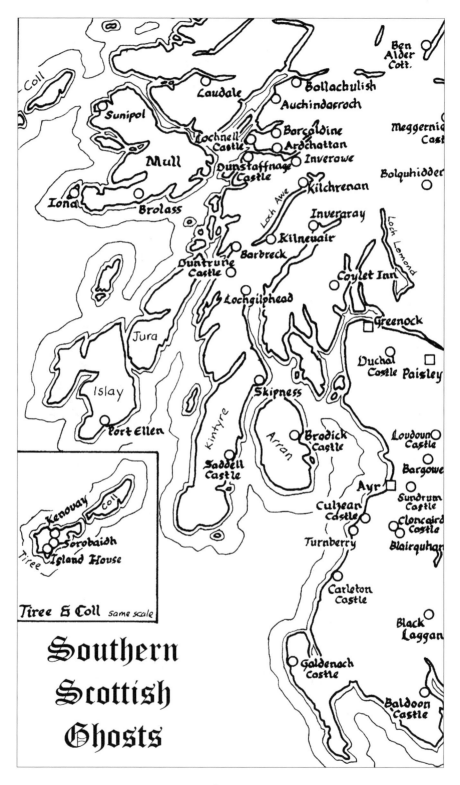

Southern
Scottish
Ghosts

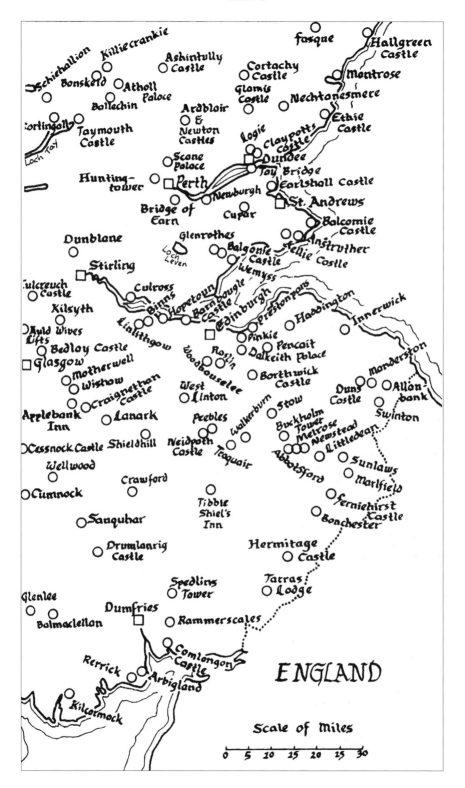

Fasque
Hallgreen
Castle

Schiehallion
Killiecrankie
Ashintully
Castle
Cortachy
Castle
Montrose

Bonskeid
Atholl
Palace
Glamis
Castle
Nechtonesmere

Fortingall
Ballechin
Ardblair
&
Newton
Castles
Ethie
Castle

Taymouth
Castle
Loch Tay
Logie
Claypotts
Castle

Scone
Palace
Dundee
Tay Bridge

Hunting-
tower
Perth
Newburgh
Earlshall Castle

Bridge of
Earn
Cupar
St. Andrews

Dunblane
Glenrothes
Balcomie
Castle

Loch
Leven
Balgonie
Castle
Anstruther
Kellie Castle

Stirling
Wemyss

Culreuch
Castle
Culross
Binns
Hopetoun
Bornbougle
Castle
Edinburgh
Prestonpans
Haddington
Innerwick

Kilsyth
Linlithgow
Pinkie

Auld Wives
Lifts
Roslin
Pencait
Dalkeith Palace
Manderston

Bedlay Castle
Woodhouselee

Glasgow
Borthwick
Castle
Duns
Castle
Allan-
bank

Motherwell
West
Linton
Stow
Swinton

Wishaw
Craignethan
Castle
Buckholm
Tower
Melrose
Newstead

Applebank
Inn
Lanark
Peebles
Walkerburn
Abbotsford
Littledean

Cessnock Castle
Shieldhill
Neidpoth
Castle
Traquair
Sunlaws

Wellwood
Crawford
Marlfield

Cumnock
Tibbie
Shiel's
Inn
Ferniehirst
Castle

Sanquhar
Bonchester

Drumlanrig
Castle
Hermitage
Castle

Spedlins
Tower
Tarras
Lodge

Glenlee
Dumfries

Balmaclellan
Rammerscales

Rerrick
Comlongon
Castle
ENGLAND

Arbigland

Kilcormock

Scale of Miles

0   5   10   15   20   25   30

9

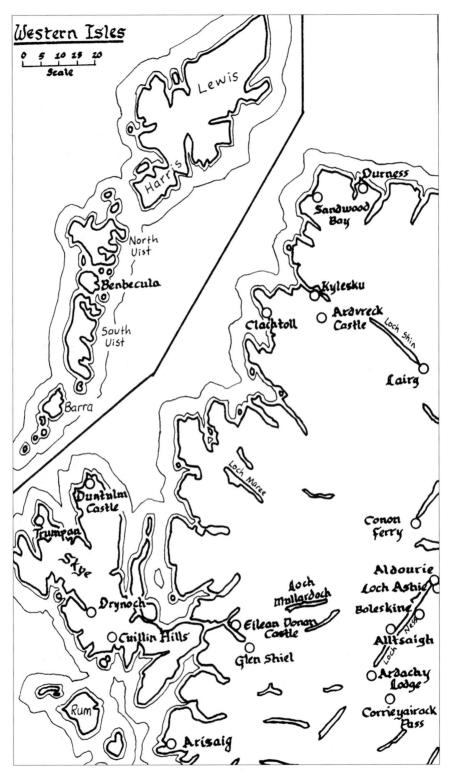

Western Isles

0 5 10 15 20
Scale

Lewis

Harris

North Uist

Benbecula

South Uist

Barra

Durness

Sandwood Bay

Kylesku

Clachtoll

Ardvreck Castle

Loch Shin

Lairg

Loch Maree

Duntulm Castle

Trumpan

Skye

Conon Ferry

Aldourie

Loch Ashie

Boleskine

Alltsaigh

Loch Ness

Drynoch

Loch Mullardoch

Eilean Donan Castle

Cuillin Hills

Glen Shiel

Ardachy Lodge

Corrieyairack Pass

Rum

Arisaig

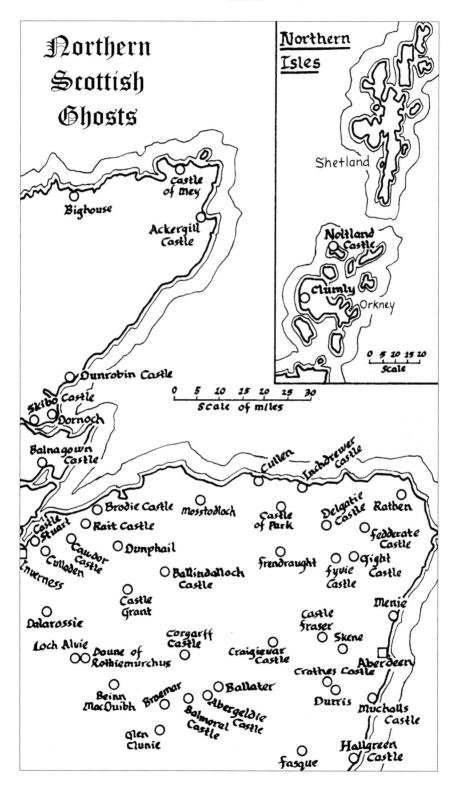

Northern Scottish Ghosts

Northern Isles

Shetland

Noltland Castle

Clumly

Orkney

0 5 10 15 20
Scale

Bighouse

Castle of Mey

Ackergill Castle

Dunrobin Castle

Skibo Castle

Dornoch

Balnagown Castle

0 5 10 15 20 25 30
Scale of miles

Cullen

Inchdrewer Castle

Brodie Castle

Mosstodloch

Castle of Park

Delgatie Castle

Rathen

Castle Stuart

Rait Castle

Cawdor Castle

Dunphail

Frendraught

Fyvie Castle

Gight Castle

Fedderate Castle

Culloden

Inverness

Ballindalloch Castle

Castle Grant

Menie

Castle Fraser

Dalarossie

Loch Alvie

Doune of Rothiemurchus

Corgarff Castle

Craigievar Castle

Skene

Aberdeen

Crathes Castle

Beinn MacQuibH

Braemar

Ballater

Abergeldie

Balmoral Castle

Durris

Mucholls Castle

Glen Clunie

Fasque

Hallgreen Castle

11

INTRODUCTION

Scotland is a land of many ghosts and spirits. Every corner of the country seems to have at least one ghost, and many haunted buildings can have half a dozen or more unexplained phenomena associated with them. Glamis Castle seems to be the haunted building *par excellence*, though the now partially demolished Ballechin House was at one time regarded as the most haunted house in the country. This book details hundreds of hauntings from every part of Scotland and from every period. Most of the old favourite stories are included, as well as numerous tales which are either less familiar or too modern to be known by the general reader.

Many of the ghost stories have certain patterns in common. The spirits are usually of a person who actually lived in the building at some time in its history. Many descriptions given of the manifestation of more recent spirits can often be identified by older folk who knew the person during their earthly life. A good number died of unnatural causes, many of them suicides or murders linked to love affairs. This seems to be one of the most common reasons for ghosts returning to haunt some location; endlessly searching for their forbidden love.

Some of the spirits are of people who are famous figures from history, like Mary Queen of Scots or Bonnie Prince Charlie. Others are just ordinary people whose souls still wander the earth in search of some type of peace. There are a number of sightings of disembodied ghosts, usually missing an arm or leg, or more often a head. Some of these arise due to a change in the floor level in the haunted castle or house, others due to parts of the body being hacked off at the time of death or murder. A fair number of animal spirits have been sighted, from black dogs and white horses to the rare monkey.

Just what causes ghosts to appear has been a subject for debate for many decades and longer. In 1894 Sir William Crookes published a paper which claimed that our souls survive the death of our physical body. He reckoned that our world had a particular wavelength, and that the spirit world existed at a different 'band'. The appearance of ghosts, poltergeists and other phenomena are said to be 'interference' between the two.

One of the most recent theories put forward by David Jones, a regular columnist for *Nature* magazine, is that ghosts exist in a spirit world whose temperature is 3 Kelvin (minus 456 degrees Fahrenheit), the same as outer space. This low temperature is said to explain why rooms suddenly turn cold when ghosts are present. Souls of the dead use body heat to make their escape; ghosts are those souls which have failed to achieve sufficient energy to make their way into the other world.

In contrast, however, Professor Trevor Stone of the Institute of Biomedical and Life Science at Glasgow University, claims that ghosts usually result from a violent death. This releases from the corpses nucleic acids that remain in the atmosphere, to be picked up by witnesses, hence 'seeing' ghosts.

I have never seen a ghost myself, but I don't doubt their existence. I have spoken to many folk who have no reason to make up a sighting, yet have witnessed something unnatural in their lives. Most relate their experiences in a matter-of-fact way, trying neither to frighten nor impress the listener, just recounting how they saw something weird as they went about their everyday life. All seem to be content with their experience, and none said that their ghost frightened them.

Readers can decide themselves whether the accounts in this book are merely tales or real-life experiences undergone by perfectly normal people. Many of the places mentioned in the text are private houses or castles, so the reader who wishes to investigate some of the stories should bear this in mind. There are, however, many haunted castles, mansions, hotels and inns that the reader may visit, and inquiries at tourist information centres will establish which buildings are open to the public.

Dane Love
Auchinleck, 2009

I

GREEN LADIES

Many ghosts seem to appear in a particular colour. Accounts of blue, white and grey ghosts are noted throughout the world, but Scotland seems to be the home of the green-coloured ghost, in particular the 'Green Lady'. Indeed just across the border in England, despite the numerous sightings of White Ladies, there are few accounts of the green variety. One possible explanation, though admittedly one with little foundation, is that the Scots ladies in question were dressed in a green tartan, which English ghosts would not be!

Tales of Green Ladies haunting ancient castles are told the length of the country, from Dumfriesshire's Comlongon Castle in the south to the Castle of Mey on the northern extremity of the mainland. Many stories link the ghost to the death of a young lover, often killed in a jealous rage by a third party.

Travelling through the country in a generally south-to-north direction, Comlongon Castle, now the property of Philip Ptolomey, is the first place where we find reference to a Green Lady. The fifteenth-century tower house is open to the public, and the adjoining Edwardian mansion has been converted into a luxury hotel. Comlongon's Green Lady is the ghost of Marion Carruthers, whose tale is recounted in a number of old Border ballads.

Marion Carruthers was being held against her will in Hermitage Castle, near Newcastleton in Roxburghshire, about which we will hear more later. It was planned that she should marry John MacMath, nephew of the Duke of Buccleuch, but she wanted nothing to do with this plan. She managed to escape from Hermitage and made her way to Comlongon, where she knew the laird, Sir Charles Murray, would look after her. He hid her in the old tower, but Marion, fearing that she was still not safe, committed suicide by jumping from an upper window. It is said that plants will not grow on the spot where she landed.

The presence of Marion Carruthers is rarely experienced at the castle, but some folk think that they have seen her and even more reckon to have heard her crying. Others claim to have felt her deathly-cold hands touching them.

At Sundrum Castle in Ayrshire we find another Green Lady. This one haunts the large castle of Sundrum, which stands above the Water of Coyle four miles east of Ayr. The castle dates in part from the mid fourteenth century, the so-called Wallace Tower having been built then, but much of the building was added over the centuries to form a long range. There are a number of secret passages within the immensely thick walls. For a time a hotel, the castle has recently been converted into a number of smaller houses.

The Green Lady of Sundrum has been spotted in the old barrel-vaulted dining room, which is located in the oldest part of the castle—the Wallace Tower. She is thought to

Comlongon Castle, Dumfriesshire, where
Marion Carruthers jumped to her death
rather than marry someone she didn't love.

be the wife of one of the Hamiltons who owned Sundrum. She has not been seen since
the castle was renovated.

South of Jedburgh in the border countryside stands the ancient tower house of
Ferniehirst, a seat of the Marquis of Lothian. Built in 1598, this castle was for many
years a favourite residence of the Scottish Youth Hostels Association but it has been
returned to its owner and restored as his home once more. A Green Lady is said to
frequent the castle, but of her history little is known. She has been seen, most often in
one of the bedrooms in the tower.

The old mansion of Woodhouselee was a seat of the Hamilton and Tyler families. The
house stood to the south of Edinburgh, and its grounds extended up the eastern foothills
of the Pentland Hills. Long in ruins, the house dated from the eighteenth century and
occupied the site of Fulford Castle. The house was demolished in 1965, save for the
stables. In differing accounts the ghost that haunted Woodhouselee has been described
as both a White and a Green Lady. Folklore has it that the apparition is that of Lady
Hamilton of Bothwellhaugh, the wife of James Hamilton of Bothwellhaugh, who
assassinated Regent Moray in Musselburgh on 23 January 1570. He then fled to France
where he supported Mary Queen of Scots' cause, before dying in 1580.

On one occasion James Hamilton was away from home when a man appeared at the
front door of Woodhouselee. He started a conversation with Lady Hamilton, persuading
her in the process that he was a friend of her husband's. She invited him in, but by the
time he reached the hall his mood had changed and he turned nasty. He stripped her
ladyship and ejected her from the house. Thrown out with her was the Hamiltons' infant
child, who died in the night as a result of the ill-treatment and the cold.

When Hamilton returned he found his wife in the garden clutching the corpse of the child, treating it and talking to it as though it was still alive. She had gone mad, and her sanity never returned. Lady Hamilton died within a short time and her ghost was often seen wandering the grounds and later, when the house fell into ruins, among the remains. The man who carried out the deed was said to have been a favourite of the Regent Moray and so was never punished for his actions.

Further north and into Edinburgh stands the very grand mansion of Caroline Park, or Royston House as it was originally known. It was built in the Franco-Scottish style at Granton between 1685 and 1696 by George MacKenzie, first Viscount Tarbat and Earl of Cromartie. Haunting the building is a Green Lady ghost, believed to be the apparition of Lady Royston, wife of Sir James Mackenzie (Lord Royston), younger son of Lord Tarbat. The ghost seems to follow a standard routine. She appears through a wall, always at midnight, and passes to the main entrance doorway where she disappears. The figure reappears in the east courtyard where she rings an old bell. This bell has been heard to toll when no one is near it, nor a breath of wind blows.

Caroline Park is also the scene of a unique phantom cannonball. Lady John Scott of Spottiswoode, who wrote *Annie Laurie*, lived here at the end of the nineteenth century. On one occasion she was in the Aurora Room when the window flew open and a solid cannonball was propelled into the room. Bouncing across the floor, it came to rest on the other side of the apartment. Lady Scott summoned her servants to come, but by the time they arrived the cannonball had disappeared. A similar incident occurred in the same room at a different time, witnessed by another person. In fact the sound of a cannonball bouncing across the floor of the room became so commonplace for a time that the residents in the house grew accustomed to it.

There is a house in Morningside, Edinburgh, which is haunted by another Green Lady. The building stands at the west end of Balcarres Street, overlooking Myreside playing fields, and is now surrounded by modern housing. In the year 1712 what was then a country house was bought by Sir Thomas Elphinstone, former governor of Maryland. He began courting a young woman, Elizabeth Pittendale, who was forty years his junior. However, Elizabeth was also friendly with an officer in the army, known as 'Jack Courage'. After a time it was decided that Elizabeth was to marry Sir Thomas, and she told Jack that they were never to see each other again. He had been posted abroad in any case. Sir Thomas and Elizabeth were married and set up home at Morningside.

By a previous marriage Sir Thomas had a son, an army colonel, who had been abroad for many months. Sir Thomas was keen for him to meet. his new stepmother and made arrangements for them to be introduced at a grand banquet. Many friends were invited, and before them all John was introduced to the new Lady Elphinstone. She was left speechless, for Sir Thomas's son was none other than 'Jack Courage'. They managed to keep up the charade of anonymity in front of the guests, but when they got a chance to be alone their love quickly developed. One day Sir Thomas entered a room and found the two kissing. In a rage he lunged at them both with a knife, and Elizabeth was killed. Sir Thomas later committed suicide.

Sir John Elphinstone leased the house to a fellow colonel and it was then that the hauntings commenced. A lady in a green dress was spotted walking along the corridor and entering what was the second colonel's bedroom. There she slumped down on the bed and cried. After a few minutes the figure disappeared. A mystic, who could converse with ghosts, was summoned and it was discovered that Elizabeth desired her coffin to be laid to rest in a vault separate from that of Sir Thomas. Her wishes were respected,

Stirling Castle, Stirling, has at least two ghosts – a Pink and a Green Lady.

and in later years when 'Jack Courage' died he was laid by her side. The Green Lady was never seen in Morningside again.

East of the capital at Musselburgh stands Pinkie House, home of another Green Lady, known as Green Jean. Often accompanied by a child, this one is rarely seen. One man was disturbed by a child a number of times but he managed to will her away, and he was never annoyed by her again.

Stirling Castle has been described by Historic Scotland as 'the grandest of all Scottish castles, both in its situation on a commanding rock outcrop and in its architecture'. There are two ghosts here, one a Pink Lady, the other Green. According to legend, when the castle was put under siege in 1303 by the English under Edward I, one of the women insisted on staying within the fortress with her husband. Edward eventually managed to take the castle, but not before the woman was smuggled across the battlements and down over the rocks. Her husband was killed in the defence of the castle, and when the woman died her spirit returned to search for him. The Pink Lady wanders through the length of the castle and as far down the rock as the church of the Holy Rude. She is most regularly seen from that part of the castle known as the Ladies' Rock.

The Green Lady, so called because of her long and flowing dress, is most commonly encountered before some major disaster. Some accounts state that she was one of Mary Queen of Scots' ladies-in-waiting. It was prophesied that the queen would die in a fire and indeed at Stirling the curtains on her four-poster bed did catch fire, probably from a candle or lantern. The lady-in-waiting managed to save the queen, but history has failed to record whether or not she perished as she did so, nor why her ghost remains at Stirling. Linked to one or other of these ghosts, or perhaps with a third spectre, are the phantom footsteps which have been heard in the governor's block. According to tradition a sentry died on duty here some time in the 1820s, and the face of the corpse was said to be terror-stricken.

Near Glenrothes in Fife stands the ancient castle of Balgonie, erected in the fourteenth century, and for many years the seat of the Earls of Leven. The castle fell into ruins in the mid nineteenth century, and the long, painstaking work of restoration is being carried out by its present owner, Raymond Morris. Since buying the castle in 1985 both he and his family have seen a number of ghosts about the castle, but the one which appears most often is a Green Lady known as Green Jeannie. She is thought to have been a daughter of the family of Lundin, who owned the castle until 1627. Little is known of how she died, or why she still appears to this day. At a recent wedding reception held in the castle, the bride told Raymond Morris that when she was a young girl of six years old she had witnessed the Green Lady walking down the stairway of the castle, then in total ruins.

There are a number of other unexplained spirits at Balgonie. The family have heard many weird noises, from voices in the great hall to footsteps in the hallways. The apparition of a white-dressed figure has also been seen in the great hall, as well as a soldier dressed in sixteenth-century uniform in the court. Those who have seen this military ghost often describe it as having one arm stretched forward, as if it was opening a door. Old plans show that there was once a wooden outhouse at the spot where this ghost appears, and that he is perhaps opening the now absent door. Other folk have seen this soldier ghost walking through the gateway to the castle.

Wemyss Castle stands on the shores of the Firth of Forth, between Kirkcaldy and Methil in Fife. For many years the seat of the Earls of Wemyss, it is now the home of the clan chief, Wemyss of that Ilk. The castle, whose oldest part dates from around 1421, boasts a 'bottle dungeon', a prison accessible only through a hole in its ceiling. The castle is haunted by a Green Lady, one of a number called Green Jean. The ghost is noted to be a wanderer, having been seen in various parts of the house, not just in a single room or in one area, as is the case with many ghosts.

Huntingtower Castle stands just to the west of Perth, which town is slowly encroaching upon the castle. Though once known as Ruthven Castle, after the Gowrie Conspiracy, when the teenage King James VI was captured and held prisoner for ten months, and a second conspiracy after which the Earl of Gowrie was beheaded, the fortress was taken into royal hands and renamed. The castle was in fact two separate buildings; the gap between the two distinct towers, just over nine feet apart, was closed when an adjunct was constructed at the close of the sixteenth century. The towers connect only at ground-floor level, but in years past this fact was overlooked by a young maiden. We can do no better than to recount the tale as told by Thomas Pennant in his *A Tour in Scotland* of 1769:

A daughter of the first Earl of Gowrie was addressed by a young gentleman of inferior rank, a frequent visitor of the family who never would give the least countenance to his suit. His lodging was in the tower, separate from that of his mistress.
[Sed vetuere patres quod non potuere vetare.]

19

Huntingtower Castle, Perthshire, is home to a Green Lady who haunts the old tower, as well as the surrounding countryside.

The lady, before the doors were shut, conveyed herself thither into her lover's apartment; but some prying duenna acquainted the Countess with it; who, cutting off, as she thought, all possibility of retreat, hastened to surprise them. The young lady's e,ars were quick; she heard the footsteps of the old Countess, ran to the top of the leads, and took a desperate leap of 9 feet 4 inches over a chasm of sixty feet, and luckily lighting on the battlements of the other tower, crept into her own bed, where her astonished mother found her, and of course apologised for the unjust suspicion. The fair daughter did not choose to repeat the leap; but, next night, eloped and was married.

The gap between the two towers has been known as the Maiden's Leap ever since.

A Green Lady, known as My Lady Greensleeves in folklore, haunts not only the castle but also the former estate that surrounds it. She is a helpful ghost, who seems to assist those in trouble. At one time there was a cottage on the estate occupied by a widow woman looking after her sick son. The boy was bedridden with a fever and a neighbour had gone to Perth to get some medicine for him. The boy was so ill that the widow feared he would die, so she set off along the Perth road to meet the neighbour. When she met her, she grabbed the medicine and hurried back to the cot-house. The boy in bed was sitting up, looking the fittest he had been for months. In fact, the fever had vanished. When the widow asked him what had happened, the boy said that a 'bonnie lady' dressed in green had touched him on the forehead and he felt better straight away.

My Lady Greensleeves also appeared at a different cottage on the estate. An old man lived there, reputedly having a secret hideaway where he kept his money. One day the cottage door was forced open and a group of armed robbers came in and demanded that he hand over his savings. The man said that he had only a few shillings in the house. The robbers did not believe him and dragged him out into the yard. As he lay on the ground he gazed towards Huntingtower. The robbers saw his face freeze with fear as he stared towards the castle. They turned round and looked at the tower house where, in a window opening, saw the manifestation of a lady dressed in green silk, her eyes brightly shining. Terrified, the robbers fled to Perth leaving the man unharmed.

Another tale recounts the appearance of the Green Lady within the castle itself. A traveller called at the castle but found Lord Gowrie was absent. Nevertheless, the housekeeper was at home and she welcomed him in. As night fell he was shown to a bedroom high in the tower. He lay in bed but was unable to sleep because of the storm that raged outside. The clock in the room ticked on and at length struck midnight. Shortly the figure of a weeping woman appeared, dressed in green, sobbing and crying. As he leaned forward to console her, the figure disappeared. On the following day the traveller set off for Perth. He was accidentally drowned in the River Tay which some folk regarded as significant.

The tale of the Green Lady that haunts Newton Castle, near Blairgowrie, has been handed down in ballad form. The story tells of Lady Jean Drummond and her attempt to win her own true love. She had fallen in love with a neighbouring laird, but his passion died and he found the affections of another. Lady Jean was extremely upset by his disappearance and set out to win his devotion again. In the upper room of the northern tower she sat for long hours trying to make herself more and more beautiful. She bought the finest satin and silk dresses and the latest leather shoes with polished silver buckles. She pleated her hair, which was long and black, with pearls. Lady Jean let her former lover see her in her finery, but still he failed to return. In a state of deep melancholy she would spend evenings in the northern tower singing morbid songs to herself.

According to tradition, after some time Lady Jean sought the advice of a fortune-teller who lived nearby. The old woman told her that fine clothes and expensive jewellery were not what was required to win her love; instead she should dress in the type of clothing worn by the fairies, called in the ballad, 'the witchin' claith o' green'. Lady Jean asked the cailleach how she was to achieve this. 'Cut a swathe of grass from the kirkyard, a branch of the rowan tree that grows on the gallows-knowe and tie them together with a pleated reed,' was the answer. 'Take them to the Cobble Pool at the gloamin' and there sit on the Corbie Stane.' Lady Jean did this, and sat for hours alone in the middle of the River Ericht. At length she heard the sound of laughter, a cold wind about her body and the feeling of hands pulling at her clothing. The eerie sensations caused her to faint. At the crowing of the cockerel in the morning, Lady Jean awoke to find herself clothed in green. The clothes were like none she had seen before, and the colour was so unusual it seemed to have many shades within it.

Lady Jean managed to win over her lover, and within a few months she and Lord Ronald were engaged. The marriage ceremony took place in the great hall of Newton Castle, and Lady Jean wore a her dress of the 'witchin'claith'. As she and Lord Ronald took their vows, the groom felt his bride's hand turn a deathly cold. He looked at her, and in her eyes he saw a dark empty gaze. Suddenly she let out an unearthly scream and collapsed at his feet. Her body was taken to the upper room and laid out on what would have been the bridal bed. She never recovered, however, and her corpse was buried on the Knockie Hill. According to the old ballad, the rude stone which marks her grave turns three times on Hallowe'en, and the ghost of Lady Jean descends to Newton Castle where her plaintive singing can be heard in the north tower.

> ...The ladye Jean comes oot frae the mools
> An' doon tae the Newton Hall.

At Ardblair Castle, which stands just one mile west of Blairgowrie, there is another Green Lady, also the victim of a doomed romance (indeed, some accounts state that the Green Ladies of Ardblair and Newton are one and the same spirit). One of the Blair sons who lived at Ardblair fell in love with Lady Jane Drummond, daughter of the Drummonds of Newton. However, the Blairs had been in a feud with the Drummonds for many years. Young Blair and Lady Jane were forbidden from meeting, and this so upset Lady Jane that she threw herself into the waters of the loch, then partially surrounding the castle, and was drowned. Her spirit travelled to Ardblair, where it continues to wander through the castle.

Accounts from those who have experienced Ardblair's Green Lady seem to put the most likely time of haunting at early evening, more commonly on a sunny day. The Green Lady passes along the castle's corridors, opening and closing doors as required. Though she makes no sound at all, the sight of her was still so terrifying that during the Second World War, when a number of evacuees were housed in the long gallery, they preferred to leave the building and risk the air raids at home. Ardblair has been the home of the Blair family since 1399 when David II granted the lands to Thomas Blair. It is now owned by the Blair-Oliphants, many of whom have reported sightings over the years.

In the same district is Ashintully Castle, which stands two miles north of Kirkmichael, itself twelve miles north of Blairgowrie. Located in Strathardle, the building dates from the latter half of the sixteenth century, when it was constructed by Andro Spalding, his coat-of-arms and the date 1583 appearing over the door. The castle has a number of ghosts—indeed it has been described as one of the most haunted houses in Scotland. Of these ghosts Green Jean, or Jane, is the best known, a former lady laird. Having inherited the castle, Jean was jealously watched by an uncle. At length he could contain his avarice no longer and one night entered the lady's dressing room where he discovered the maid combing Lady Jean's hair. Not expecting the lady-in-waiting to be present, he had to murder both women, and tradition states that he disposed of the maid's body by hiding it within a large chimney. This chimney was for years noted for its poor drawing qualities. The uncle dragged the corpse of Jean, who had been wearing a green dress, down the staircase and disposed of it. However, her ghost has often returned to haunt the castle, and not only appears as a Green Lady, but also in the form of phantom footsteps echoing through the castle's hallways. One of the most common locations at which she appears is the walled graveyard that stands amid trees near to the castle. There the greedy uncle had erected a memorial to his niece, and it is by the side of it that her figure is seen.

The second ghost of Ashintully is that of 'Crooked Davie', who haunts the drive to the castle. Davie was employed by the Spaldings as a messenger, and despite his deformed back, he was fast on his feet. On one occasion he was sent to Edinburgh with a very important message. Davie had a girlfriend at Ashintully, one of the maids, so he was even more keen than usual to hurry back. In fact, he made it to Edinburgh and back within the same day. Returning to Ashintully, he was so exhausted that he fell asleep by the fire in the great hall as he waited Spalding's return. When the laird did arrive home', he spotted Davie fast asleep, with papers hanging out of his pocket. In a rage, thinking that he had not yet set out for Edinburgh, he slew him on the spot. It turned out that the papers were in fact the answer to Spalding's letter.. The ghost of 'Crooked Davie' is said to wander along the lanes around Ashintully, seeking revenge on the Spalding family.

A third ghost associated with the castle is that of a tinker, supposedly with the name of Robertson. He arrived on the grounds one day and the laird had him hanged on the Dule Tree for trespassing. Before he died the tinker cursed the family, saying that the Spaldings of Ashintully would die out. His spirit is still seen on occasion.

Still in Perthshire, in the holiday resort of Pitlochry, stands the massive pile of the Atholl Palace Hotel. The hotel is a huge baronial edifice located at the south-eastern side of the town. One of the hotel's towers is the haunt of a Green Lady who has scared residents here since Victorian times. To prevent guests being disturbed by the ghost, which was happening on a regular basis, the room was eventually converted into a staff bedroom. Undaunted, the Green Lady continued to make appearances. Hotel guests in adjoining rooms began to make sightings where previously none had been recorded The hotel even went to the length of calling in a local minister to have the spirit exorcized but whether this has worked it is too soon to tell.

Muchalls Castle was built between Aberdeen and Stonehaven by Alexander Burnett of Leys, who had just completed Crathes Castle. Muchalls was to be his second home, his residence by the sea. It was his son, Sir Thomas, who completed the building in 1627. Both Muchalls and Crathes have the honour of being haunted by Green Ladies, but different ones.

Muchalls has a secret stairway within the castle and a legend of a smugglers' tunnel from the building to the Gin Shore. The Green Lady who haunts the castle has been described as young in appearance. She has manifested a number of times over the last century, one of the more recent sightings being in the 1970s. On that occasion a castle guest entered the dining room on the upper floor and obtained a glimpse of the lady facing the wall. However, within seconds, the apparition in her lime-coloured dress disappeared. According to tradition, this phantom is thought to be of a young girl who drowned at the castle end of the smugglers' tunnel.

Crathes is a far better-known castle than Muchalls, and is now in the care of the National Trust for Scotland. The tower was constructed between 1553 and 1596 by Archibald Burnett and remained in that family's hands until it was passed over to the Trust in 1951 by Sir James Burnett. However, the family retained the right to live in the Queen Anne wing.

On the third floor of the tower is an apartment known as the Green Lady's Room where an apparition has been seen crossing from one side to the other. At the fireplace she lifts a baby and both figures then tend to disappear. Among many witnesses of this Green Lady the most famous is undoubtedly Queen Victoria, who saw the two figures whilst visiting the castle. Sightings of the ghost have been connected with a death in the Burnett family, the spirit appearing as a death herald.

Tradition states that the Green Lady of Crathes formerly haunted the castle that stood on an island in the Loch of Leys, the Burnett home before Crathes was built. And yet

Crathes Castle, Kincardineshire, where Queen Victoria is supposed to have witnessed the apparition that haunts the Green Lady's Room.

there is another intriguing twist to the tale which seems to link the ghosts inextricably with Crathes. During renovation work to the Green Lady's Room, workmen lifted the hearth at the fireplace and discovered skeletons of a woman and child. That the bodies were hidden would tend to indicate that they had both been murdered, but another variant of the story states that the woman herself had been the murderess, driven to the deed to fulfil a jealous ambition.

Not far from Crathes stands Durris House, attached to a small tower built in the early seventeenth century on the site of an earlier castle. The older house was haunted by a Green Lady, or at least its grounds were. According to tradition, this Green Lady only appeared to men, women being unable to see her. The story centres on the Fraser laird's wife. The Marquis of Montrose arrived at Durris where he stayed with his friend. The two men were· of different political beliefs, and as the night wore on the arguments grew more heated. The lady at first tried' to quell the two, but at length placed a curse on Montrose and his army. As a result, the Marquis had Durris House burned and the cattle and horses killed. The date of the fire was 17 March 1645. The Lady wandered around the ruins the next day, crying loudly and wringing her hands. After a while she heard the sound of the burn murmuring softly amid the trees of the Den of Durris. She lowered herself into the water and there found her rest.

There are two castles in Aberdeenshire which have Green Ladies. Menie is today a mainly Victorian neo-baronial mansion house of the 1840s, but at its core there survives part of a fifteenth century castle. It is located near Balmedie, ten miles north of

Fyvie Castle, Aberdeenshire, is the home of a Green Lady who came back to haunt her ex-husband on his second wedding night.

the county town. In the basement of the original castle a Green Lady has been sighted walking around during the hours of nightfall. Fortunately for the castle residents she is noted as being of a friendly nature.

Fyvie Castle, like Crathes, is one of the National Trust for Scotland's finest treasures. Located near the Aberdeenshire village of the same name, Fyvie was bought from Sir Andrew Forbes-Leith in 1984. The castle has five towers, each named after one of the families that owned Fyvie. The Green Lady that haunts the castle is thought to be Lilias Drummond, second wife of Alexander Seton, first Earl of Dunfermline, who bought Fyvie from the Meldrums in 1596. When Lilias died, some say by starvation, Lord Dunfermline waited only four months before marrying the youthful Grizel Leslie. During the second night of their honeymoon, which was spent in the castle, the newlyweds were disturbed throughout the night by scraping and scratching sounds outside their window. Come morning, the curtains were drawn to reveal the name 'D LILIES DRVMMOND' scored into the window sill. The name, written upside-down in letters three inches tall, can still be seen outside the Drummond Room's northern window.

Moving north-west of Fyvie, across the River Deveron and into Banffshire, brings us to the small village of Cornhill, eight miles from the county town. Here stands the Castle of Park, an old Z-plan tower-house of 1536 to which various additions have been made. In the grounds of the castle, long a seat of the Gordons of Park, who took part in the Jacobite rebellion, the Duke of Cumberland's army camped on his return south after Culloden. The castle is now open to guests for meals or accommodation and organizes murder mystery evenings. But nothing is more mysterious than the castle ghost.

The Green Lady of Park is said to have been a girl who became pregnant while in service at the house. She was dismissed from her job and subsequently hanged herself. Her apparition has been seen numerous times, mostly in the grounds, though some folk, including the Gordon owners, have seen her looking from a second floor bedroom window in the castle.

The Castle of Park is also haunted by a monk who, according to legend, was walled-up in a ground-floor room. A recent owner of the castle, James Duncan, had seen both ghosts, but told me he had never felt anything sinister about them. He also saw misty shapes moving across rooms and disappearing into walls, and on a number of occasions certain items went missing only to reappear at a later date. Mr Duncan also related that in the top floor of the four-storey tower, the room can suddenly change from hot to cold and back again, within a matter of minutes.

Another Banffshire castle is Ballindalloch, a very fine example of Scots baronial architecture. The main tower dates from around 1546 and has been the seat of the Grants and Macpherson-Grants since 1499. The castle, which is open to the public during the summer months, boasts at least three ghosts, one of them a Green Lady, the second also female, and the third General James Grant. The latter died in 1806 and was buried, as was his wish, near the Mains, but it is said that his apparition still rides' around the estate on a white charger every night. He then returns to Ballindalloch, where he has been seen walking the dungeon passage at the foot of the original tower. Here is located the castle wine cellar, originally the prison, whose heavy door is still secured with an enormous lock. Beneath the cellar is supposed to be a pit-prison, whose only opening is in the ceiling, but this was filled up in the great flood of 1829, which left four feet of silt and gravel on the castle holm.

The Green Lady of Ballindalloch supposedly haunts the dining-room, though she makes few appearances. The dining-room was originally the great hall of the oldest part of the castle. Directly over it is the Pink Tower, a bedroom, which both Lady Macpherson-Grant and Mrs Russell regard independently as the most haunted room in the building. However, standing there myself, I was unable to sense any unnatural atmosphere.

The other female ghost at Ballindalloch is seen on the Bridge of Avon. It is said that she was a daughter of the house who had a lover that spurned her advances. Nevertheless, she is said to cross the bridge every evening from Ballindalloch to Bridge of Avon post office with a letter to send to him. When the old bridge was bypassed by the present river crossing, the workmen engaged in the construction are said to have witnessed her on several occasions.

Three miles north of Wick, overlooking Sinclair's Bay, stands the imposing edifice of Ackergill Tower. Erected in 1475, the castle is home to a Green Lady, also known as the Beauty of Braemore. Helen Gunn lived at Braemore, a remote clachan or township on the banks of the Berriedale Water in Caithness. She was engaged to be married, but had a secret admirer in Dugald Keith. On the night before she was due to marry, Dugald arrived at her parents' home and kidnapped her, taking her back to Ackergill. She was pestered by Dugald to give up her fiancé and marry him, but she resolutely refused. After being imprisoned for some time she took her own life by leaping from the battlements. At the castle there is a stone in the ground marking the spot where her body landed. Some folk claim to have seen the manifestation of the Beauty standing on the battlements, looking over the wide bay. This incident probably took place in the

Ballindalloch Castle, Banffshire, where at least three ghosts, including a Green Lady, have been experienced.

Castle of Mey, the former home of the Queen Elizabeth, the Queen Mother, where the Green Lady haunts Lady Fanny's Room.

fifteenth century, for it is noted that in 1518 Keith of Ackergill and his son were killed by the Gunns in retribution for an 'ancient wrong'.

Almost as far north as it is possible to go on the mainland of Scotland stands the Castle of Mey, just six miles from John o' Groats. Known for a time as Barrogil Castle, the Green Lady here haunts the uppermost room in the old tower. Known as Lady Fanny's Room, the apartment contains the unusual feature of a walled-up window, whose origin dates back to the sixteenth century. The fifth Earl of Caithness had a daughter of whom he was very proud. However, she fell in love with a ploughboy who worked on Barrogil home farm. When her father caught wind of the romance he took the girl and locked her up in the highest chamber of the castle. The girl was wont to sit by the window and gaze at her suitor at work in the fields of Barrogil. When her father became aware that the girl was spending her time in this way, he hired a mason to block off the window, leaving just one other opening that faced in a different direction. The girl was not to be outdone, however, for she soon discovered that she could lean quite far out of the window and still catch a glimpse of the plough boy. This was to be her final act, for one day she leaned too far and plummeted from the window to her death. The ghost of the girl haunts the Castle of Mey as the Green Lady, and a number of people have experienced her presence. The castle was in danger of demolition until it was bought and restored by Queen Elizabeth, the Queen Mother, in 1953. A number of workmen involved in the restoration also claim to have seen the spectre.

Heading west from Mey we arrive at the crofting village of Melvich, just over the border into Sutherland. Here, on a promontory in the Halladale River near its confluence with the sea at Melvich Bay, stands the large lodge known as Bighouse, or An Tigh Mar, erected around 1800. The Green Lady of the lodge is said to be the spirit of a woman who hanged herself in her bedroom a century ago. Why she did so is not known, but it is said that she appears most often in the apartment where she took her life. Others say that she is also seen throughout the house passing through walls as though nothing was there.

The imposing edifice of Inverawe House stands to the east of Taynuilt, at the foot of the mountain range of Cruachan Beann in Argyll. It is actually a tower house of the fourteenth century or earlier to which various extensions have been added over the years. A Campbell stronghold, Inverawe was one of the many places visited by Mary, Queen of Scots. She is said to have dined on salmon here. There are two ghosts at Inverawe, one of a Highlander, the other of a lady known as 'Green Jean'. She is believed to be the ghost of Mary Cameron of Callart (which is near North Ballachulish, on the shores of Loch Leven), who married the laird.

According to legend, Mary was engaged to Diarmaid Campbell when a serious outbreak of plague struck the Cameron household. Tradition has it that the pestilence arrived when a Spanish ship, loaded with goods, was trading along the west coast of Scotland. Everyone in the house, from the laird down to the servants, perished, save for poor Mary, who had been locked in her room as a punishment. Her hunger growing, Mary remained in her room for a couple of days, wondering why the house had been plunged into total silence. At length a man, Donald Cameron, arrived with orders to burn the house to rid it of the plague. Mary called to him that she was still alive, but he was afraid to let her out in case she too had the illness. He agreed, however, to take a message to Inverawe. Diarmaid came with the speed of a deer, bringing with him a new dress for Mary. He carried her to the shore where she washed in the salty water. The house of Callart, along with its rich furnishings, was then razed to the ground.

Campbell took Mary Cameron, who was in a weak condition, back to Inverawe, but his father refused to allow either of them into the house, for fear of spreading the plague still further. For the next few months they took shelter in a cave near Inverawe, until Diarmaid's father was satisfied that all signs of the sickness had gone. Mary's strength gradually returned, and the two were married. They went on to bring up a large family, but Diarmaid died in 1645 of wounds received at the Battle of Inverlochy and was buried at Ardchattan Priory. When Mary died her spirit remained at Inverawe, haunting the house in a friendly way. It is said that she has helped many people throughout the centuries although some have been frightened by her appearance.

Inverawe has a second ghost, that of Duncan Campbell. (His brother, some say cousin, was Donald Campbell, victim of the Appin murder, of which more later.) One day Duncan received a visitor who claimed sanctuary at the house. He told his host that he had killed a man, but not whom. Three nights he spent at the house and for three nights Duncan's sleep was disturbed by the spirit of his brother telling him that his guest had killed him. Highland hospitality was such that a guest in your house could not be ill-treated. Finally, the spirit told Duncan to 'Meet me in Ticonderoga.' He did not know at the time where this was, but years later in 1758 he was in America with the Black Watch. He was killed in battle on 17 July near a fort occupied by the French, named Ticonderoga. He is buried at Fort Edward in Canada.

Far south in the county of Argyll, on the peninsula of Kintyre, stands Skipness House. A replacement for the ancient Skipness Castle, the house was long owned by the Campbell, then Graham, families. Here, in the south-east tower, lived a brownie ghost, or *gruagach* in Gaelic, that would assist the servants. She had long golden hair. Mrs Barton, at one time the housekeeper, had her own room within the castle. She would often tell how the Green lady would help her to feed the hens in the evening. A Mrs Higginson collected folk tales from the district, and in her manuscript, kept at the School of Scottish Studies at the University of Edinburgh, she records the following description:

> She was very small, just like a child in stature. She wore a green silk dress. She had neither shoes nor stockings on. She would help Mrs Barton to tidy up her house. When the Campbells would be away from home, a night or two before they returned the Green Lady would be working in the house, setting it in order for their homecoming.... A brother of Mrs Barton's attended [a ball in the castle] to help the servants, but early in the evening he felt unwell and he went to bed in Mrs Barton's room. Everyone seems to have been so busy no-one looked near him until the ball was over and then he was found nearly dead in bed. The Green Lady nearly killed him for being in Mrs Barton's bed. She was boxing him all night. They took him to his home in Lochranza. He never recovered from the thrashing the Green Lady gave him. He died very shortly after.

A later owner of the country house was Angus Graham, a noted historian, who died in 1980. His sister, Mrs Vaughan Johnson, witnessed what might have been the Green Lady. She had taken her young daughter into the first-floor room of the tower. Whilst there she noticed a face at the open door, looking round the left-hand doorjamb. It was positioned as if the spirit was standing on the bottom step outside the room and peering in to try and have a look at the child. On closer inspection Mrs Johnson found that no one was there.

2

COUNTRY HOUSES

There are many tales linking ghosts and haunted goings-on with castles the length and breadth of the country, or as Burns said, 'Frae Maidenkirk tae Johnnie Groats.' However, there are fewer associations with the later country houses and mansions. There are a number, however, and the following pages will detail these hauntings.

In the border country stood the house known as Allanbank, located a few miles south of Chirnside, and for many years a seat of the Stuart family. The resident ghost is believed to be that of a former girlfriend of Sir Robert Stuart, created first Baronet of Allanbank in 1687. On one occasion Robert Stuart (still to be knighted) was in Paris and there made the acquaintance of a beautiful young girl called Jean or Jeanne. Some accounts state that she was a Sister of Charity and that Robert persuaded her to leave that order. Others say that she was a Flemish Jew or even an Italian. In any case, the two were a couple whilst Robert was in France, but after a time he began to tire of her affections. He returned to Scotland where, after some months, he met another woman and made plans to wed.

Jean missed Robert so much that she made arrangements to journey to Scotland, where at length she arrived in Berwickshire. Somehow she found out that Robert was engaged to be married and that the wedding was to take place in the near future. She made haste to Allanbank, where Robert and his fiancee were just leaving in a horse and carriage. In a fit of anguish she hurled herself in front of the horses and was trampled to death.

The first person to see the ghost of Jean was Robert Stuart himself. One day he was returning from business when he spotted a woman standing up on the arched gateway to his house. He drew up his carriage to get a closer look and was horrified to find that it was the ghostly figure of Jean, dressed in a long lace dress, blood I streaming from her head. The ghost was named 'Pearlin' Jean', 'pearling' being a Scots word for a type of lace of silk.

The spectre of Jean was apparently a common sight at Allanbank, and various accounts have been given of sightings over many years. Jean would go about the house in high-heeled shoes, opening and closing doors in the middle of the night. It was also said that if the portrait of Jean, which had been painted, was placed on the wall between those of Robert and his wife then the hauntings stopped. However, the painting must normally have been hung elsewhere, for the ghost was noted by many people. In fact servants in the house grew so accustomed to the appearance of Pearlin' Jean that it left them unaffected.

In the 1790s the Stuarts leased Allanbank to another family which did not know about the existence of the ghost. This state of ignorance did not last long, however, for within a few days two ladies who shared the same bedroom were woken in the night by a noisy phantom wandering back and forth in the room. The ghost remained there all night and the guests were unable to sleep. The next day, after recounting their experience to the servants, they were told of Pearlin' Jean. One of the rooms, the room in which the ghost was most commonly seen, was actually left unused for many years. The last Baronet of Allanbank had to have the contents of the house sold off.

Seven different ministers from the district were summoned to exorcize the ghost, but each one failed in the task. Whether or not this eventually led to the demolition of Allanbank is not known, but the mansion was razed in the first half of the nineteenth century, and the ghost seems finally to have departed. An old woman in the neighbourhood is supposed to have enquired, 'Where will Pearlin' Jean gang noo when the hoose is dismolished?'

Near Kelso is located the country-house hotel of Marlfield, or Marlfield-on-Kale, east of Eckford. Incorporating an ancient castle at its core, the biggest proportion of the house dates from the mid eighteenth century and is distinguished by its twin gables. No one has seen the ghost of Marlfield, nor has any idea of the earthly person to whom the spirit belonged, but many have experienced it passing them by. The ghost has a habit of squeezing past various folk, most often in the stillroom or else in the passageway leading to the ladies' toilets. These parts of the house are close to the entrance of an old tunnel or hiding-place, the history of which is not known. It may have been an escape route from the old castle, or perhaps a cubby-hole where Roman Catholic priests lay low during the Jacobite uprisings. Of the folk who have experienced the ghostly sensation, the list includes Ann Taylor, wife of the owner, and the hotel's head waitress.

Abbotsford was the home of Sir Walter Scott, a mansion built by him on the site of Cartleyhole farm. This name was distorted to 'Clarty hole' by the locals, which means 'dirty hole'. The house was built over a period of time, many of its architectural features based on older Scots buildings. The ghost of Sir Walter himself is said to haunt the building, as well as the ghost of George Bullock.

Bullock was in charge of the construction of Abbotsford on Scott's behalf and he also made a number of pieces of furniture for it; the oak table and sideboard in the dining-room were crafted by him. Soon after he died in 1818 his ghost appeared at Abbotsford, and has been seen repeatedly over the years. Sir Walter experienced Bullock's unearthly presence at the very hour of his death, noting 'violent noises' within the building. He actually got up from his bed and walked through the house carrying an old claymore, but could find nothing amiss. During later alterations to Abbotsford the ghost of Bullock appeared again, though on most occasions only the sound is heard.

The apparition of Sir Walter Scott himself has often been seen at Abbotsford. The house formed so much of Scott's life that it would be strange for his spirit td leave it in death. At the height of his fame Scott built the house from the proceeds of his poems and novels. Shortly afterwards he became a partner in the publishing house of Constable. When the firm collapsed, he was left with debts of £100,000, and the house was under threat of being sold off. Scott managed to avert this, however, by a concentrated spate of work writing novels by the shelf-load, usually in the library where his desk can still be seen. When he died in 1832 he owed not one penny.

The ghost of the great novelist is usually seen in the dining-room which overlooks the Tweed. It was here that Scott died in bed. The house is open to the public and a number of visitors have reported sighting the ghost.

Abbotsford House, Roxburghshire, where the ghost of the great novelist, Sir Walter Scott, has been witnessed a number of times.

Farther upstream on the River Tweed, near Innerleithen, stands the ancient pile of Traquair House, according to some, the oldest inhabited dwelling in Scotland. The house, which resembles a French château, was originally a Royal hunting lodge, and many kings have visited over the centuries. It has been calculated that twenty-seven reigning monarchs have stayed at Traquair. The estate was granted to James Stuart in 1491 and the same family, now Maxwell-Stuart, have owned it ever since.

There are two ghosts at Traquair, one male, the other female. The male ghost, thought to be of Bonnie Prince Charlie, is most often seen on the avenue leading from the house to the Bear Gates. This avenue was once the original entrance drive to the house, but tradition has it that following Prince Charles's exit from Traquair the then laird, the fifth Earl of Traquair, announced that the gates would remain closed until there was another Stuart on the throne of Scotland. Prince Charlie was unsuccessful in his attempt to win the crown, and the gates have stayed shut ever since.

The other Traquair ghost is thought to be of Lady Louisa Stuart, sister of the eighth and last Earl of Traquair. She actually inherited the estate on his death in 1861 and became acquainted with both Robert Burns and Sir Walter Scott. She was 100 years old when she died in 1875, and the apparition of an old woman has often been seen wandering the grounds.

Andrew Brown, who worked on the estate, saw the Lady in the early 1900s and gave such an accurate description of her that the older folk in the district were able to confirm the spirit's identity. He also met a descendant of Lady Louisa's dressmaker who still had some samples of material that matched the ghost's dress. Andrew Brown had been

Traquair House, Peeblesshire, has two main ghosts – one an old lady, the other believed to be of Bonnie Prince Charlie.

working in the joiner's shop on the estate when he noticed an old woman pass by the doorway. He moved out to gain a closer look and was amazed to see her walk through two locked gateways. There is a portrait in Traquair of Lady Louisa reading a gook and Lady Louisa's Walk extends from the house downstream alongside the Quair Water.

Manderston, which stands just over a mile east of Duns in Berwickshire, is one of the greatest Edwardian mansions in Scotland. It is said that Sir James Miller had the house built in 1903 to the best standards possible in order to impress Lord Scarsdale, his father-in-law, who resided at Kedleston Hall in Derbyshire. A number of distinguished features of Kedleston were copied, and no expense was spared in its construction. It is said that when the architect, John Kinross, asked Miller what sort of budget he should work to, he was told, 'It doesn't really matter—there is no limit.'

One of Manderston's noblest features is the grand staircase, the balustrade of which is silver-plated. Modelled on the stairway in the Petit Trianon at Versailles, home of Louis XIV and Madame de Pompadour, it was restored in recent years, the silver replated and the whole thing polished. It is on this staircase that Manderston's ghost can be seen, a woman in Edwardian dress. Some say that the lady was Sir James Miller's widow, Eveline, Lady Miller. Miller himself died in 1906, aged forty-one. They had only been married for thirteen years.

On the south side of Edinburgh stands Dalkeith House, or Palace as it is better known. Used as a residential study centre by Wisconsin University, the house is still owned by the Duke of Buccleuch, as is the parkland which surrounds it. The palace is home to some form of supernatural presence that always occurs at the same spot, near to the double doors of an upper drawing-room. Nothing is ever seen, but dogs are known to be very wary of this spot, and their hair stands on end. Among those who have experienced eerie sensations there is Her Royal Highness Princess Alice, Duchess of Gloucester, who spent much of her childhood at Dalkeith, she being a daughter of the seventh Duke of Buccleuch.

Another palace, and one with a greater right to be called such, being a royal residence, is the Palace of Holyroodhouse, located at the foot of the Royal Mile in Edinburgh. Started by James IV in the fifteenth century, the building has· undergone numerous extensions and alterations over the centuries. It is still the official residence of the royal family when in Scotland. The palace has been the scene of many notable events in the history of Scotland, not least the murder of David Rizzio in 1566. He is thought to have been a lover of Mary Queen of Scots, whose husband, Lord Darnley, was found murdered a year later.

It is these two murders that form the background to Holyroodhouse's main ghostly presences. In the room used by Darnley as an audience chamber unusual shadows are often experienced. One of the senior members of staff was at work in that room when he noticed a shadow at the foot of the door to the stairway. Thinking there was someone behind, he opened the door, but despite a thorough search was unable to find the cause of it.

The Long Gallery is located on the first floor along the northside of the courtyard and is decorated with 111 portraits of Scottish monarchs. A magnificent room, 140 feet long, it is haunted by ghostly footsteps. These have been heard right up to modem times, and are the most common manifestations experienced in the palace. A window cleaner is also said to have seen a figure in the gallery from his ladder on the outside of the palace.

Holyroodhouse is also the home of the ghost of a Grey Lady. Who this ghost represents is not known, but it is speculated that she was one of Mary Queen of Scots' ladies-in-waiting. The figure is usually very faint and appears in Queen Mary's audience chamber.

To the west of Edinburgh, on the edge of the ancient town of Linlithgow, stands a third palace. Linlithgow Palace has been a royal residence since·the twelfth century but was destroyed by fire after the Battle of Falkirk in 1746. Itis now protected by Historic Scotland and is regularly open to the public. King James V was born here, and it was he who had the great hall added to the structure in the 1530s. James V was a great lover of Linlithgow, and spent a great deal of time here. He married Mary of Guise, who so loved the palace that she claimed it was more 'princely than any of the chateaux in the whole of France'. When she died her ghost remained at Linlithgow, supposedly in Queen Margaret's bower, awaiting James V's return.

A second ghost haunts Linlithgow, and is usually seen near to the entrance porch. The Blue Lady walks from here down towards the parish church of St Michael where she disappears. Most sightings of her have occurred in April and September, usually at nine o'clock in the morning.

A few miles from Linlithgow stands the Binns, a country house now in the care of the National Trust for Scotland. The Binns was the ancestral seat of the Dalyell family, the infamous Sir Tam Dalyell, or Dalziel as it is sometimes spelled, though always pronounced De-ell, being a colourful character from Scottish history. He fought at the Battle of Worcester in 1645, where he was taken prisoner. He managed to make his escape and joined the royalist cause. He became commander of the Scottish forces in 1666 and raised the Scots Greys regiment in 1681. Dalyell is credited as being the person who introduced thumbscrews to Scotland. He became noted as a persecutor of the Covenanters (who called him 'Bluidy Dalyell'), and rumours of his being in league with the Devil originated from this time. It was said that he and the Devil had played cards on a number of occasions. Auld Nick was soundly beaten in one of these games, and in a fit of rage threw the card table into the pond. When the pool dried up in the summer of 1878 a large marble-topped table was found at the bottom! It is now back on show in the house. Running down from the Binns to the Forth at Blackness there is reputed to be a tunnel, much used when smuggling was rife. The Binns was built in the seventeenth century but was later recased in a castellated manner. Given to the Trust in 1944, the Dalyell family still takes an active role in its maintenance.

The House of the Binns, to give the mansion its full title, has a number of ghosts. The spectre of Sir Tam Dalyell has been seen riding on horseback from the Black Lodge, across the old bridge which crosses the Errack Burn, and up to the house. Dalyell dismounts from his grey horse right in the middle of the present dining-room, which was built on the site of the former stable courtyard. His ghost has also been seen riding through the woods to the summit of the nearby hill, surmounted by a tall folly. It is said that the Dayells and the nearby Hopes of Hopetoun had a bet on who could spend £20 in the most useless way, and this was the Dalyell bid.

Another ghost seen at the Binns takes the form of an old man, dressed in a long brown cloak, who gathers firewood from the grounds; there is also a water spirit that lures unsuspecting travellers to their death by drowning.

A few miles east of the Binns stands Hopetoun House, one of the largest country houses in Scotland. The seat of the Marquess of Linlithgow, Hopetoun was erected from 1696 onwards and is regularly open to the public; The ghost here is usually seen wandering the grounds, most often along a particular pathway. The spirit is usually dressed in a long dark cloak, and some reckon that it is a death herald, foretelling a bereavement in the Hope family. This track is often spurned by dogs.

Another large country house boasting a ghost is Scone Palace, seat of the Earls of Mansfield. Erected in 1803, the mansion is home to a manifestation that has been dubbed 'the Boring Walker'. Rarely seen, the spirit produces foot-step noises within the south passage. These are quite unusual, however, because the phantom's feet sound as if they are walking on stone, whereas the corridor has floorboards.

In Dundee halfway to Lochee, there used to stand Logie House, which was demolished early in the twentieth century. It was owned by the Read family, and following the death of Fletcher Read in 1807 stories began to circulate about a Black Lady that haunted the house. The figure was black in more than one sense, for she was supposed to have been an Indian princess captured by Read whilst working with the East India Company. Read had brought her to Scotland as his wife, but kept her locked up in the house. For decades tales of the ghost were passed around Dundee, each one more sinister than the last.

One of the most celebrated haunted houses in Scotland was Ballechin, which stood in Strathtay to the east of Aberfeldy. Dating from 1806, most of the house was demolished, leaving to survive only one wing of 1884. Long owned by the Steuart or Stewart family it gained a local reputation for being haunted in the late nineteenth century. In August 1896 the trustees of Captain Steuart let out the house to a wealthy family who wanted to use it as a shooting lodge. They had paid for the year's lease in advance, but after seven weeks in residence were so terrified by the goings-on that they fled from the, house, forfeiting their tenancy.

The previous owner of the house, Captain Steuart's uncle, Major Robert Steuart, died in 1876. He was known as an eccentric and would often recount his wish to come back after death. He predicted that his spirit would return in the form of his favourite dog, a black spaniel. Some say that one of his dying wishes was for his body to be fed to his dogs. After his death the rest of the family ensured that all fourteen of his dogs were shot! Nevertheless, strange occurrences took place. The smell of dogs would pervade the house, and residents found themselves menaced by an invisible force, one with an unmistakably canine aura. Inexplicable sounds were also heard, from the sound of arguing and knocking to footsteps and small explosions.

Captain John Steuart died in January 1895, and it is said that he heard three loud knocks at the house just before setting off to London. He had been discussing estate business in his study when the sounds were heard, but was unaware that they were a warning signal, heralding his death. On arrival in London he was knocked down by a cab and killed.

Word of the hauntings reached the Marquis of Bute, a keen historian and member of the Psychical Research Society. He, Major Le Mesurier Taylor, Miss Ada Goodrich Freer and other members of the society took the lease of the house with the intention of conducting on-the-spot investigations. They invited thirty-five guests to a country-house party and later asked them to recount all the noises and sounds which they heard. Amongst these were the sounds of shuffling feet, thuds on the panelling and talking. More interesting were the' accounts of a hunchback mounting the stairs, witnessed by two guests, and the many reports of a large black spaniel throughout the house. During the investigation an Ouija board was produced and using 'automatic writing' they managed to find out the names of long-forgotten people in portraits on the walls.

There have also been reports of ghostly nuns at Ballechin, often appearing by the small burn which flows from Dunfallandy Hill nearby. Major Steuart's sister Isabella, who died in 1880, had been a nun.

The hauntings witnessed at Ballechin were detailed in a book entitled *The Alleged Haunting of B—House, Perthshire, During the Tenancy of Colonel Taylor,* written by John, Marquis of Bute and Miss Ada Goodrich Freer. Published in 1899, a reprint appeared the next year. Letters on the subject appeared in *The Times* in June 1897, written by Andrew Lang, EH.W. Myers and Lord Onslow. In 1892 a Jesuit priest, Father Hayden, witnessed loud inexplicable noises whilst trying to sleep at Ballechin. In 1932 the house was sold to a Mr Wemyss Honeyman and on his death in 1963 was partially demolished.

A few miles west of Pitlochry, in the lovely Glen of Tummel, lies Bonskeid House, until 2001 a YMCA hostel. At one time, according to the tales, the house was haunted by a poltergeist that would throw objects around the rooms, from burning peat to a full spinning-wheel. It was said that the mysterious happenings ceased when a servant woman was thrown out of the house and told not to return.

The Gladstone family have owned Fasque from 1829 until 2008, the most noted member being William Ewart Gladstone, four times prime minister of the United Kingdom during the Victorian era. The estate lies on the south side of the Grampian Highlands, near to Fettercairn in Kincardineshire. The house has been described by the previous resident, Peter Gladstone, as 'the most haunted house I know'.

One frequent manifestation is the spirit of Sir Thomas Gladstone, elder brother of the prime minister. Another ghost is reckoned to be of MacBean, a butler—this identification is based on the fact that the ghost, like he, is lefthanded. The spirits seem to be present in every room in the mansion, but are rarely seen.

In Aberdeenshire, a few miles from the market town of Huntly, stands Frendraught House, an ancient mansion built around an older castle. This was the scene of a celebrated fire in 1630, when the Viscount Frendraught, John, Viscount Aboyne, John Gordon of Rothiemay, English Will, Colonel Ivat and others including servants were killed. The fire was said to have been deliberate, the result of a feud between the Crichtons of Frendraught and the Gordons, but an investigatory commission which sat in April 1631 failed to pinpoint the blame, yet stated that 'the fire could not have happened accidentally, but designedly'. The local folk, however, reckoned that Lady Elizabeth Crichton was to blame; and a ballad recalls her part in the massacre. She moved to nearby Kinnairdy Castle, but when she died her spirit returned to Frendraught.

One of the earliest-known sightings took place in the eighteenth century, when a 'dark woman in a white dress' was reported. She had been seen in both the house and the surrounding beechwoods. In 1838 a local man, William Thomas, spotted the ghost's face at the window at a time when he knew that the house should have been empty. He called over the gamekeeper, who also witnessed the face, and together they broke into the house through a kitchen window to find out who was there. Despite a thorough search of the mansion, armed with shotguns, they could find no one inside, nor any signs of a forced entry.

Tradition states that the ghost of Frendraught cannot be seen by the laird, and the present laird, Morison of Bognie, has not witnessed any unnatural occurrences. However, his wife, Yvonne Morison, has experienced the ghost. On 28 October 1948 she was alone in the house when she was aware of footsteps descending the stairway towards the basement kitchen where she was working. Terrified, she walked slowly towards the doorway to the hall and called out to the ghost to show itself. But it did not, and the footsteps ceased. Those who have seen the ghost usually describe it as dressed in a white dress, edged with gold. It most often appears on the stairways within the house.

Guests of the Morisons at Frendraught have also experienced unnatural happenings. On two separate occasions a similar haunting has taken place, and at both times the visitors have cut short their stay. At night, after retiring to bed, the guests have heard the sound of arguing, fighting and crashing sounds. They were a bit embarrassed by this, thinking that the Morisons were quarrelling, but later discovered that the wall separating the two bedrooms was eight feet thick, and no noise could pass through it.

Cullen House in Banffshire stands a mile or so inland from the beautiful fishing village of the same name. The house is really an old tower of 1600, now divided into lesser dwellings. The estate, as well as Old Cullen House, still remains in the hands of the Earl of Seafield, whose family have owned it for generations. Cullen House is haunted by the spirit of the third Earl of Seafield, known in history as the 'Mad Earl'.

James Ogilvie, third Earl, inherited the estates in 1764 but gained a reputation for being insane. On 3 November 1770, whilst mentally unstable and unaware of what he was doing, he murdered his best friend. Later, when he regained his reason, he was so overcome by remorse that he committed suicide. Although laid to rest in the family vault, his ghost returned to wander through the old house.

Many people have seen the Mad Earl's spirit over the centuries—most commonly when large social events were held at Cullen House. The library, pulpit and church rooms are where he most often appears. In 1964 two journalists doing an article on ghosts visited the house. Sceptics when they went in, both experienced a horrible aura in the house and heard the sound of footsteps behind them.

Up Strathspey to Aviemore we come to the Doune of Rothiemurchus, a small country house that is the Grant seat on Rothiemurchus estate. The oldest part dates from the late eighteenth century and was home to Elizabeth Grant (1797–1885), author of *Memoirs of a Highland Lady*. The house has a room that for many years was never used by the family because no one was able to get a good night's sleep there. An oddly-shaped room, it was kept furnished but rarely used. At one time a shooting tenant leased the house and one of the guests reckoned that he could stay in it quite safely. However, during the night he was startled by a strange sound. He went out of the room to investigate, but could find no source for the noise. When he returned to the room it was icy cold and plunged in total darkness. As he groped for the lamps, he knocked his head and fell to the floor unconscious.

According to tradition, the house was haunted by the spirit of a son of the laird who lived some time in the eighteenth century. This boy was deranged, and was locked up for hours on end in this particular room. One day he managed to make his escape from his prison and met a servant girl on the stairway. In his overwrought state he strangled the girl and then threw himself to his death over the balustrade. His spirit has remained in the house ever since, mostly in that bedroom.

Heading westwards we arrive at Loch Ness where the house of Boleskine stands on the eastern shores, near to the village of Foyers. Situated on an afforested hillside, the house was built in the late eighteenth century by the Hon. Archibald Fraser, a kinsman of Lord Lovat. The house was sold by the Frasers at the beginning of the twentieth century to Aleister Crowley (1875–1947), self-styled as 'the wickedest man in the world'. It was purchased in the 1970s by Jimmy Page, guitarist with the rock group Led Zeppelin, but was sold by him in 1990.

Boleskine houses a number of evil spirits, including a poltergeist—various objects have been noticed to vanish and reappear later. Crowley has been blamed· for these occurrences, although he himself experienced ghostly happenings. He was notorious for performing Satanic rites and sacrifices at Boleskine, and tradition states that a tunnel extended from the house to the nearby kirkyard, which contains the ruins of the old parish kirk. This place is said to be haunted by witches. Crowley had been interested in evil spirits since childhood and rumours abound in the district of his weird behaviour. He is said to have had a mistress who lived on the opposite shore of Loch Ness, at Grotaig.

Another haunted house by Ness-side is Ardachy Lodge, located by the side of the River Tarff, just over a mile from Fort Augustus. In 1952, when Peter MacEwan bought the lodge, he appointed the MacDonald family to look after the house. Shortly after arriving, the MacDonalds witnessed an old lady in the building, and would often see her crawling along the hallways. It turned out that the previous owner of the lodge had been a Mrs Brewin, an eccentric who was known to move about the dwelling on all-fours. The MacEwens sold the lodge and it was later demolished.

On the other side of Loch Ness, in Glen Cannich, is the hydro-electric dam of Loch Mullardoch. Sometime in the 1980s two climbers were descending from the mountains towards the loch. They headed for a large house that they could see from the slopes, but at one point they dropped into a gully to cross a mountain stream. When they climbed up the other side they were amazed to discover that the house had disappeared. Wondering what had happened, they discussed their vision with others on their return home. It turns out that the loch was formerly much smaller, and that between 1947 and 1951 the dam was constructed, raising the water level by 116 feet and in the process engulfing the former Benula shooting lodge. Although it has not been seen since, the climbers were convinced that this is the building they saw.

The main road south from Loch Ness leads through Fort William and across Loch Leven at the Ballachulish Bridge. At Ballachulish, a collection of villages constructed around the old slate-mining industry, stands Ballachulish House, erected in the eighteenth century to replace an older house that burned down in 1746. A selection of spirits haunt the building.

One of the ghosts seen is of a Highlander on horseback, though his former identity is not known. What is certain, however, is that at Ballachulish House Captain Robert Campbell was given the order to kill all the MacDonalds of Glencoe under the age of seventy. The infamous massacre of 1692 took place in the nearby glen. A second ghost who wanders throughout the house is of a little old lady. She has been identified as Sophia Boulton, wife of Samuel Boulton, latterly Sir Samuel, first Baronet, who lived here for a time. Sophia Boulton died in 1900.

Sophia Boulton used to conjure up the image of her ideal house which became known as 'mother's dream home' by her family. When the Boultons went to view Ballachulish the house turned out to be exactly as Mrs Boulton had dreamed. She could guide her family through every room on their first visit. The Boultons bought the house and remained there for some time. Sophia Boulton's ghost still frequents her 'dream home'.

Five miles along the Oban road from Ballachulish is the village of Duror, near which is the house of Auchindarroch. An old building of two storeys, it was, like Ballachulish, constructed by one of the branches of Stewart of Appin. Here the Maid of Glen Duror wanders throughout the building, opening and closing doors, moving ornaments and other items. Indeed, one room was named the Haunted Room because inexplicable happenings occurred there so often. The woman is thought to be the ghost of a MacColl who looked after the family in Auchindarroch. Numerous modem sightings of her have taken place and many of the Stewarts living in the, house have seen her.

Continuing south on the Oban road we circle round Loch Creran and enter the Barcaldine Forest. By the side of the Dearg Abhainn, which means red river, stands Barcaldine House, another of the many large dwellings with which the Argyll coast seems to be covered. This was a Campbell seat, whose oldest part dated back to the sixteenth century. It was rebuilt in 1896 and restored in 1988 as a hotel and holiday centre. There are two ghosts in the house, one a Highlander the other a Blue Lady.

The Highlander is thought to be the Red Fox, Colin Campbell of Glenure, who was murdered on 14 May 1752. This is one of the most famous tales of the Scottish Highlands, fictionalized in *Kidnapped* by Robert Louis Stevenson. There is still doubt over the murderer's identity. Stewarts and Campbells were at feud for a number of years, which led to the murder of the Red Fox in Lettermore Wood a mile or so to the west of Ballachulish Bridge. A memorial cairn marks the spot. Allan Breac Stewart was immediately suspected, but he had just fled to France. A few days beforehand he had stayed with his kinsman, James Stewart of the Glens, at Acharn, who had given him money and clothes for the trip. James Stewart was arrested and tried at Inveraray for being 'art and part' to the murder. He was later hanged at Ballachulish, where a memorial on a rocky knoll at the southern end of the bridge marks the site of the gallows.

Though James Stewart was not guilty of the actual murder, he was hanged for his part in the preparation, according to Sir James Fergusson in *The White Hind*, despite counter-claims that the jury was biased, being composed of eleven Campbells out of fifteen, with the Duke of Argyll as a judge. Who it was that actually committed the murder has never been proven. Some say that Allan Breac was innocent, and there have been many theories advanced over the years. Itis said that some folk!, descendants of the original perpetrator, know the name, which has been handed down in secrecy from that day to this.

The Red Fox haunts Barcaldine House because it was here that his corpse was laid for a time prior to his interment at Ardchattan Priory, located to the south on the other side of the hills. His ghost has often been spotted by visitors to the house as well as tourists walking in the glen.

The Blue Lady of Barcaldine tends only to be seen in the house. She is clearly a music lover, for each time her apparition is spotted there is usually some form of music being played.

Ardchattan Priory itself is haunted. Located through Gleann Salach from Barcaldine House, the priory overlooks Loch Etive. Little of the Valliscaulian Priory of 1230 remains, most of the building having been incorporated into a country house of 1847, still home to a branch of the Campbells. The manifestation of a nun is said to wander around the buildings. According to tradition, one of the monks of Ardchattan had a nun from Kilmaronaig Convent brought secretly to the priory, where she was hidden beneath the floorboards of the oratory. She is said to have come out to join him on some nights, but died of asphyxiation in her hiding place.

On the southern shore of sea-loch Sunart, in Morvern in Argyll, stands Laudale House. A simple, yet attractive three-storey building, it is said to be haunted by the ghost of Angus Mór, murderer of Donald Madan. Madan was the infant chief of the Madans of Mingarry and Angus Mór Madan was his uncle and guardian. He was also his heir at the time, and it was his avarice that led him to murder. As young Madan crossed a ford en route to his wedding Angus Mór shot him with an arrow. However, one of the groom's party spotted the figure in the bushes and identified him as Angus Mór. This precipitated a battle between the Camerons of Locheil (young Donald's bride-to-be was the chief's daughter) and the Macleans of Ardgour against the Macleans of Duart and Angus Mór's followers. This took place at Leac na Saighde in Gleann Dubh, near Kinlochaline. Angus Mór was shot by an arrow and died on Tom Aonghais Ruaidh— Red Angus's Hill—and the Cameron forces soundly defeated the Macleans of Duart. Angus Mór's body was taken down Glen Laudale to Laudale House, where it was laid in a cellar for a number of days.

Though Angus Mór was entitled to burial in the kirkyard at Kilchoan, that was where young Donald Madan was interred, and it was felt that the two should not be buried in the same place. After a time it was decided that the corpse should be buried at Keil in Lochaline, where a large memorial stone depicting a knight in armour used to mark his grave.

At Laudale House the sound of something heavy being dragged across the floor can be heard, but nothing can ever be found to cause such a noise. It is said to be Angus Mór's body being dragged from the cellar to the boat that transported it round the coast to its final place of rest.

Another country house in Argyll is Barbreck, located by the side of the Barbreck River at the head of Loch Craignish, twenty-two miles south of Oban. In the surrounding countryside the vision of a young woman with long hair has been seen a number of times. She is usually dressed in a dark tartan skirt and has a veil or hood over her head, hiding her face. If anyone approaches her as she sits quietly on a rock outcrop she usually disappears.

Island House stands on a promontory by the shore of Loch an Eilein, midway between Heylipol and Crossapol on the island of Tiree. It was built in 1748 by the Earl of Argyll and incorporates the remnants of an old castle that was a seat of the MacLeans of Tiree. The castle originally sat on an island in the loch but when Island House was being constructed the factor, a MacLaren, ordered the islanders to transport loads of rubble to build a causeway to the island. One of those forced into working for MacLaren was a poor crofter from Barrapol who had to borrow a neighbour's cart to do the job. As he was finishing his labours one evening the factor arrived on the scene and ordered him to bring one last cartload before retiring for the night. The crofter protested, saying that he was tired and that he would start work again the next morning. MacLaren said no, and that if he did not bring another load then he would be thrown out of his croft. The man could do nothing else but obey the factor, but as he wearily set off he warned the factor that he would not spend a single night in his new house.

The factor later took ill, and as he lay in bed he remembered the crofter's warning. He ordered his men to carry him in his blanket to Island House, but as he was carried through the door he breathed his last. The ghost of MacLaren haunts the house to this day.

Island House is also home of a guardian fairy which is believed to be a little lady dressed in green. She is rarely seen, but the proprietor of the house in the 1970s has heard her moving furniture. On one occasion he was downstairs and heard chairs and tables being moved around above him. Thinking that it was his son, who was in his bedroom on the second floor, he went up to find out what was going on. The boy was discovered lying in bed and he immediately asked his father why he was moving furniture around in the kitchen? The middle floor was checked, but nothing had been moved, and no one else was present.

Another strange phenomenon associated with the house is the appearance of lights at the windows. These usually occur when no one is at home, and when investigated are. found not to come from any of the electric lights in the building. Indeed, on one occasion it was later realized that the position of the lit window did not match any of the present window openings and might, in fact, have been one of the original castle windows long since bricked up.

Shieldhill House is an ancient mansion located at Quothquan, north of Biggar in Lanarkshire. Indeed it is now operated as a hotel, whose proprietor claims the foundation date as 1199. That year the Chancellor family acquired the castle, and remained in ownership until 1959. One of the daughters of this family is said to be the Grey Lady that haunts the building.

According to one tradition the girl was raped by a soldier during the 'Killing Times' of the second half of the seventeenth century. This was a period when Charles II tried to impose Episcopacy on the Scots and many were killed for refusing to adhere to his wishes. Others say that she fell in love with a lowly farm-hand. In any case, she became pregnant and in shame the family had her locked up in what is known as the Glencoe

Room. When the child was born it was taken from her and left to die in a field. The Chancellor girl never recovered from the experience, and when she died her spirit remained at Shieldhill. A number of people have seen her walking on a section of flat roof of the building, and her manifestation has appeared many times in the Culloden Room and Chancellor Suite of the hotel. Occurring more often is the sound of footsteps or bumps in the night.

On the eastern moors of Ayrshire, near to Muirkirk, stood Wellwood House, built in 1878 by Colonel John G.A. Baird. It incorporated an old baronial house which had been built by the Campbells in 1600. This building was haunted by a ghost called 'Beenie'. As with many female ghosts, Beenie is said to have loved a man but was murdered by a third party. Her room was in the original part of Wellwood House, and she is said to have walked from the house to the Lang Plantain where she cried and wrung her hands. Should anyone disturb her the ghost disappears back towards the house.

Beenie may have been murdered in the house itself, perhaps on the stairway, for there existed for many years a stone step marked with bloodstains. The servants of the house were often asked to scrub the marks off, but when the stone dried the patches returned as fresh as ever. A mason was instructed to remove the stone and replace it with another. Within a few hours of doing the job, the mason died mysteriously, and the stains appeared in the new tread. Wellwood House was demolished in 1926 and the ghost of Beenie seems finally to have been laid to rest.

Glenlee house stands to the north-west of New Galloway, in the Stewartry of Kirkcudbright. It is haunted by a Grey Lady, reputed to be the manifestation of Lady Ashburton. Some folks say that Lady Ashburton poisoned her husband, whereas others think that the butler murdered her in the same way as part of a scheme to steal some valuable antiques. There is an old account of some of the supernatural happenings at Glenlee:

Mrs S—, who is still alive, tells how the grey lady appeared to her one evening as she was sitting in front of her dressing-glass, waiting on her maid to come and do up her hair. While looking into the mirror she became aware of some-one or something behind her, and then saw a lady enter by the door of her room, pass across the floor, and disappear through a door which communicated with a dressing-room. As the house was full of company at the time, she wondered whether some of the strangers had mistaken the way to her room, but she waited in vain for her return, and just as she was thinking of going to explore the mystery, it occurred to her that there had been no sound of doors opening or of footfalls on the floor, nor was there any sound in the direction in which the lady had disappeared, and finally it struck her that the lady was not dressed like anyone in the house. All this passed through her mind in less time than it takes to tell it, and when examination was made for this strange and unaccountable lady, she was nowhere to be found.

Meanwhile, I must inform the reader that Mrs S— at this time knew nothing of the ghost story connected with the Park, and so she said nothing of the apparition which had disturbed her for fear of being laughed at, but she could not get the affair out of her mind. Some time afterwards she was calling at Kenmure Castle, and inquired of the lady of the house whether there was any story of Glenlee being haunted, or whether anything had ever been seen there of recent years. Lady G— replied that Lady Ashburton was said to walk about in a grey silk dress, and that some even reported that they had heard the rustle of it as she passed on her ghostly way.... On another occasion Mrs S— was sitting up with Mr S—, who was seriously ill, and during the night a kind of rap was heard on the door or about the door which roused her to go and see what it was. Upon opening the door a face stared at her, but spoke not, and passed silently along the dimly-lighted corridor out of sight.

On another occasion Captain Kennedy was leaving Glenlee when he remembered that he had forgotten something. He ran upstairs to his bedroom and on entering spotted the woman at his dressing-table. Thinking it was one of the guests still in the house, he withdrew, but on returning to his coach, discovered that all had been accounted for.

Arbigland House stands above the shores of the Nith estuary 13 miles south of Dumfries. Within the estate is the cottage where John Paul Jones was born in 1747, later to be founder of the American Navy. Arbigland House was at one time owned by the Craik family and a daughter of the house fell in love with a groom named Dunn. This romance being below her station, she was the subject of gossip in many circles. After a while Dunn mysteriously disappeared, said to have committed suicide; but according to others he was murdered by one or more of Miss Craik's brothers to prevent the allegiance with their sister. Miss Craik was so overcome with grief that she ran away from home never to be seen again, except in spirit form. Known as the 'Ghost of the Three Crossroads', she has appeared many times around the estate, and rather less frequently in the house itself.

Rammerscales is a rather unusual mansion that stands on the slopes of the Tinwald Hills, three miles or so from Lochmaben in Dumfriesshire. It is unusual in appearance, being a foursquare Grecian block, rising three storeys above a cellar, the roof fairly flat and surrounded by a balustrade. The house thus seems to be rather tall, like an ancient castle dressed up in a classical guise.

Rammerscales was the home of James Mounsey, chief physician to the Russian Empire. However, following the assassination of Czar Peter in 1762, he knew that he was in danger, having been the Czar's personal doctor. He left the country and after a time arrived at his newly-built Dumfriesshire mansion. There had already been attempts on his life, the most recent having been at Leith docks as he disembarked from his ship. At Rammerscales he was always in fear of attack and at length, in 1764, arranged for his funeral to take place, and published notices of his death in the papers, hoping that his Russian assailants would then leave him alone. Rammerscales was altered so that each room had at least two doors of escape and extra stairs were installed. He lived on at Rammerscales for another nine years, dying in 1773.

Mounsey's ghost remained in the building where the new owners, the Bell-Macdonalds, christened it 'Old Jacobus'. The manifestation appeared a number of times, most often in the library, which had been Mounsey's favourite room. During the Second World War the house was occupied by a teacher and pupils from Glasgow, but they were so frightened by the ghost that they preferred to live in the stables thereafter.

3

SOLDIERS AND BATTLEFIELDS

There are several spirits and ghosts found in Scotland that appear as soldiers or warriors. If ghosts are apparitions of people who were killed or died tragically, then soldiers who fell in battle seem to be a logical origin for the phenomena.

Perhaps the earliest recorded soldiers to have inhabited Scotland were Roman. Cnaeus Julius Agricola led a massive army across Europe and arrived in this northern part of Britain in around 79 or 80 AD. However, the Romans were forever being terrorized by the different local tribes. As a result Hadrian's Wall was erected from the Solway to the Tyne in 118 AD to keep the Caledonians out. The Antonine Wall was erected in around 140 as the Romans tried to push their frontiers further north, but because of the many attacks sustained, the fortification was abandoned and Hadrian's Wall refortified.

It is from the period when the countryside between the two walls was occupied by the Roman army that the ghosts seen at Crawford in Lanarkshire originate. The Roman road that pushed up Annandale, across the Beattock Summit where a large camp was formed, and thence down Clydesdale passed through what is now the village of Crawford. The Main Street formed part of the road, but over the years the level of the road surface has been raised by the addition of further layers of gravel, cobbles and ultimately tarmacadam. It is for this reason that the ten Roman legionnaires which have on occasion been seen marching down the thoroughfare are only visible from the knees up. The reason for ghosts being only partly visible, as mentioned in several accounts, is that ceilings and floors have often been lowered after the spirit was of this life.

At Bonchester Bridge in the border countries another phantom Roman army has been seen. They follow the line of an old Roman road which linked Bonchester with Chesters, now the A6088. This roadway was a branch of Dere Street.

Another sighting of supernatural Romans in the border country has taken place at Newstead, near to Melrose. It was here that Dere Street crossed the Tweed, and an important Roman fortification was established beneath the three summits of the Eildon Hills, hence its Roman name of Trimontium. There have been a good many hauntings here, though few folk have actually seen the spirits. What is experienced are the sounds of the Roman settlement, hammering, banging and sawing, as if they were busy constructing their homes and shelters. The sound of a bugler announcing commands to the soldiers has sometimes been heard, as has the tramp of marching feet. Most of those who have heard the noises have done so in the early evening, when all is still around them.

Roman soldiers have also been seen in sprit form at Dunblane in Perthshire by the author Archie McKerracher. In 1974 he stood outside his house on the outskirts of the town to get some fresh air. It was a dark night, and he could hear the sound of many tramping feet. Over a period of twenty minutes or so the sound seemed to get louder and louder, as though an army was marching past. It did not bother him, though, for he returned inside and went to bed.

A week later Archie McKerracher was visiting and elderly couple who lived on the same estate. They told him that their cat and dog had been frightened by something in the past week, and gazed across the room as though they were watching something. Their evident unease lasted twenty minutes. Further discussion elicited the fact that the animals must have witnessed the scene at the same time as McKerracher. A third witness turned up ten years later when he was giving a lecture on local history. Cecilia Moore had sensed the army marching through her front garden.

Research revealed the fact that in 117 AD, the Ninth Hispana Legion had marched through the Dunblane area on the way to putting down a Celtic uprising. They seem to have disappeared in the area, whether killed in a battle or not was never discovered. The housing estate was also known to have been built over two Roman marching camps, and comparison of aerial photographs of the site before development with those after showed that the Roman road passed right through the gardens of the houses concerned.

In the ancient history of Scotland tales 'of battles between clan chiefs abound. Some say they are the stuff of legend, but no doubt there are some factual origins. The tales of Ossian and Fionn MacCumhaill have left the truth so far behind that they are regarded by some as purely fictional, yet these folk probably once lived. Near to Loch Ashie in Inverness-shire, six miles south-west by south of the capital of the Highlands, Fionn MacCumhaill is said to have fought a pitched battle with some of the Highland clans. Others claim that he was warring with invading Norsemen. Some say that every year at daybreak on May Day the battle is re-enacted by ghosts of the soldiers.

In the 1870s a number of people witnessed the battle taking place, but instead of pronouncing it the work of the Fingalian hero, they claimed, unconvincingly, that the apparition was a trick of the light. It was said that the image was a global reflection of a battle in-the Franco-Prussian War. A traveller also experienced the battle scene during the First World War, yet despite the fierce fighting in evidence not a sound was heard nor a trace of the conflict left once the ghosts disappeared.

A battle with a more historical basis is that which took place at Nechtanesmere, near Forfar, on 20 May 685. Here, between Letham and Forfar is Dunnichen Hill on whose slopes King Brude mac Beli of the Picts defeated the Angle forces under Egfrith. The warriors taking part in the battle have been seen a number of times, most notably by Miss E.P. Smith in 1950, who was forced to walk home to Letham after her car skidded off the road.

Miss Smith spotted some flaming torches in the distance, carried by figures wearing primitive dress. Some of them walked in a curve across the present-day fields perhaps following what would have been the shore of the ancient loch of Nechtanesmere. Miss Smith sensed that the men were searching for their slain comrades, for they were bending down and turning over corpses to examine their faces. If unrecognized the body would be left to lie. Miss Smith's dog also seems to have experienced something menacing for just as Miss Smith saw the soldiers the dog began to growl.

The ruins of Dunphail Castle stand in the grounds of Dunphail House, seven miles south of Forres in Moray. The castle was in ancient times a seat of the Comyn or Cumming family, who owned most of the right bank of the River Fmdhorn. Indeed, the Gordon-Cummings still live at Altyre and have extensive grounds here. The left bank of the Findhorn was, and is, owned by the Earls of Moray. Back in the first half of the fourteenth century the lands of Darnaway Forest were bestowed on Thomas Randolph, first Earl of Moray, by his uncle, King Robert the Bruce. The Earl died in 1331. The Cummings and Morays were at this time at feud over the right to hunt in Darnaway Forest. The Morays claimed this as their sole privilege, but the Cummings argued that they had hunting rights before the Morays arrived, being hereditary foresters of Darnaway. Alasdair Cumming led a force of 1,000 men to attack Darnaway, but word reached their opposition before they could attack the castle. The Morays set an ambush at a gorge half a mile south of Darnaway and managed to drive the Cummings back towards Dunphail. In the retreat Cumming was forced to jump for his life across the Findhorn, a spot known ever since as Randolph's Leap.

The Cummings were then besieged in Dunphail. After starving them for a few days, the Morays lit fires around the building and asphyxiated those inside. Many were killed and it is said that their heads were fixed on to spikes on the castle battlements. The ghosts of headless soldiers have been seen in the castle several times since, and on other occasions only the heads have been visible. One can also reputedly hear the clashing of swords and the dying groans of the soldiers within the walls.

A headless horseman has been witnessed, roaming about the island of Mull. He is regarded as a harbinger of doom for whenever he appears a death occurs In the Maclaine or MacLean families. According to the old story he was Eoghan a' Chinn Bhig (Ewan the little-head), son of John Maclaine, fifth chief of Lochbuie. One evening in 1538 he was out riding his horse when he came across an old woman washing clothes in a mountain stream. As he approached her he could see that the clothes were shirts that were drenched in blood. Eoghan realized straight away that the woman was a herald of death, yet he still resolved to take part in the battle planned for the next day, against the MacLeans of Duart. As expected, Ewan was killed in the field, an enemy soldier cutting off his head with a broad Lochaber axe. The old woman was never seen thereafter, but the headless horseman has taken her place.

Many have seen the ghost of Eoghan over the last 450 years, and he was sighted regularly in. the second half of the nineteenth century, sometimes with his large black hound by his side. Sometimes the dog has been seen alone, as in 1909 when Murdoch Maclaine died. It is said that the headless horseman has also been seen on the island of Coll, at one time also owned by the MacLeans.

In 1615 a feud had broken out between the Campbells and MacDonalds, as seemed always to be the case. Duntrune Castle was a Campbell seat, but the Macdonalds under Colla Ciotach (Colkitto, or left-handed Coll) attacked it. Previously he had sent his piper forward to spy out the lie of the land and the best way of taking the castle. Pipers were privileged in years past, and he was made welcome in the castle. After a few hours his motives were put under suspicion, so the Campbells imprisoned him in one of the turrets. The Macdonalds waited for a while but became impatient and decided to attack the castle in any case. From his prison cell the piper saw the galleys approaching and on his pipes played a tune known as 'The Piper's Warning to his Master':

Coll, my beloved, avoid the tower, avoid the dun,
Coll, my beloved, avoid the, Sound, avoid the Sound,
I am in their hands, I am in their hands.

The Macdonalds caught wind of the pipes and undestanding their meaning postponed their attack. The Campbells also heard the music and taking the piper from his jail cut off all his fingers. The musician was unable to survive the loss of blood and the shock. His corpse was buried below a large slab in the kitchen, but his ghost is said to haunt the turret room. He also strikes up a strange knocking on doors and the sound of footsteps has been heard in the building. Ghostly pipe music is heard more frequently and for a time objects were thrown around some of the rooms. When once the castle was being refurbished, the skeleton of a man minus his fingers was found and the Dean of Argyll laid the body to rest at last. The Campbells sold the castle to the Malcolms in 1792, which family still reside there.

Ghost soldiers have been seen on the island of Skye. Some say they are also Macdonalds, though others claim them to be MacLeods, both families having owned extensive lands on the island at one time. They are known to the locals as 'The Silent Ones', and have been seen on various roads on the island over the years. Some reckon that there are about fifty members of the party, but as they march along no sound is ever heard. From which period in history the soldiers originated is unknown, though some say that their uniforms are Jacobite. Half-brothers Peter Zinovieff and Patrick Skipworth are among the many folk who have seen these soldiers. Camping at the foot of the Cuillin mountains in November 1956, at 3 a.m. they opened the tent door to see a group of kilted soldiers rushing across the moor. On the following night they experienced the same scene, though this time it was one hour later.

A tale of a military drummer linked to Edinburgh Castle originated in 1650. One night a soldier on sentry duty heard the sound of a drumbeat from the castle esplanade. He went to look and there saw a drummer marching up and down, beating out a sombre rhythm on his instrument. The sentry challenged him, but when no reply was forthcoming he fired a shot from his musket. When others came to his aid, the drummer could not be found. The next night a different sentry was put on duty, and he too heard the drumming. Yet again nothing could be found when help was summoned. The situation persisted for several evenings, and even the castle governor, Colonel Walter Dundas, heard the sound of armour and ghostly footsteps.

The ghostly drummer is reckoned to have been a warning to the garrison that the castle was about to be attacked. It all came true in September 1650, when Cromwell's soldiers put the castle under siege and after three months forced a surrender from Dundas and his men. The ghost has been seen since, some folk claiming that it is headless, though more often only the sound of the drumbeat is heard.

A phantom piper has links with the castle, too. According to a Victorian tale, a forgotten tunnel was discovered in the castle some time in the early nineteenth century. Tradition had it that there was one which extended down the Royal Mile from the castle to the Palace of Holyroodhouse, and people reckoned that this was it. It was decided that the best way of plotting the route followed by the tunnel was to send a piper into it, playing his Instrument en route. The rest of the party would then follow the sound of the pipes from above, and map out the direction on their charts. The piper was duly sent into the tunnel, and the surveyors began plotting the route from above. However, half-way down the High Street the sound of the pipes suddenly stopped, and the piper was never seen again—or at least not in the flesh, for some folk claim to have seen a ghost playing the pipes at various points along the spine of Edinburgh from the castle to the palace.

Between the years 1637 and 1689 there was much bloodshed in the southern half of Scotland over the right to worship as one liked. The Covenanters fought against the imposition of Episcopacy on Scotland by kings Charles I and II, many dying on the moors and in prisons for their belief in religious freedom. The government employed many soldiers and dragoons to search for these hill-men, who were forced to hold services, or conventicles, on the moors, and put them to the sword. One of their most notorious persecutors was Sir Andrew Bruce of Earlshall, known by the Covenanters as 'Bloody Bruce'. He is known to have martyred four men on Lochenkit Moor in Galloway in 1685 and to have taken part in the Battle of Airds Moss in East Ayrshire in 1680.

Bruce's castle, Earlshall, stands in attractive gardens near to Leuchars in Fife. A Z-plan tower house, it was erected In 1546. Bruce's ghost has been noted here, as well as a number of other weird occurrences. The sound heavy footsteps, apparently Bruce's, has been heard on one of the spiral staircases.

Other spirits at Earlshall include that of an old woman, thought to have been a servant in the castle. On one of the beds a depression forms itself, as though some invisible being is lying there. Objects have been noted to move from spot to spot, and some say that they have felt invisible hands touching them. In the garden at Earlshall is a particular area into which dogs are frightened to enter.

Another persecutor of the Covenanters lived at Buckholm Tower near Galashiels. The ruins of this fortified house stand on a hillside to the north of the town in the border country. Erected by the Pringle family in 1582, by the late seventeenth century the castle was owned by another Pringle. He was a wife-batterer and at length his spouse and ten-year-old son ran away from home, never to return. Pringle turned his attentions to routing out the Covenanters. One day he was out with his two hounds on Ladhope Moor, where a conventicle was in progress. However word reached the hill-men and most of them had fled by the time the persecutor had arrived. Only an old man, George Elliot, and his son remained, the old man being too weak to run. Pringle took them prisoner and locked them up in his vault at Buckholm. Rather than confess to where the Covenanters had fled, they preferred to take their own lives, hanging themselves from iron hooks affixed to the ceiling.

Elliot's wife arrived at Buckholm within a few hours, threatening to kill Pringle if he would not free her husband and son. When he took her down to the vault he was dumbfounded to find their corpses hanging from the hooks like carcasses of meat. The wife cursed Pringle for causing the death of her two men, pledging that he would find no peace on earth or in the life hereafter.

Within a short time Pringle died a torturous death, and his ghost remained at Buckholm. It is said that every June, on the anniversary of his death, his spirit and those of his two wild dogs appear at the old castle. The hounds are heard howling and the laird's ghost is heard shouting out for mercy. Some say that the hounds are evil spirits that seek out Pringles in revenge for setting his dogs upon the two Covenanters.

The Jacobites took part in a battle at Killiecrankie 2½ miles north-west of Pitlochry in Perthshire. Here they defeated the soldiers of William III under General Hugh MacKay

Eilean Donan Castle, Ross & Cromarty, has experienced the appearance of ghostly soldiers, perhaps emanating from the Battle of Glenshiel.

on 27 July 1689, but not before losing their leader, Graham of Claverhouse, or 'Bonnie Dundee' who is buried in the vault at Old Blair kirk, near Blair Atholl. The Pass of Killiecrankie, where much of the action took place, is today owned by the National Trust for Scotland and a visitors' centre tells the story of the affray. Also in Trust hands is the Soldier's Leap, a narrow gorge where one of the men managed to leap the River Garry to safety.

The battle scene of Killiecrankie has been most commonly experienced as a red light or glow that seems to appear on the anniversary of the engagement, though others have witnessed the whole clash re-enacted before them. The red light is said to have been seen by John Graham, Viscount Dundee, as he slept in his bed the night before the battle. During the hours of darkness he saw the light, then a man appeared at the foot of his bed blood dripping from his head. Dundee woke up, but his guard assured him that no one had entered the tent all night. The experience is said to have signalled Dundee's death.

A second account exists of the ghost of Bonnie Dundee. At Edinburgh Castle Lord Balcarres was in charge of the Jacobite prisoners who were held there. One night in 1689 he retired to his quarters, drew back the curtain on his four-poster bed, and saw lying there the figure of John Graham. Lord Balcarres asked him what he was doing, but there was no reply, and after a few moments the figure disappeared. Perplexed, Lord Balcarres went to sleep, but next morning word reached him that Graham of Dundee

Inveraray Castle, Argyll, has a number of ghosts, notably of some soldiers who were killed in the Jacobite wars.

had been killed at Killiecrankie. Dundee's ghost is seen from time to time at the castle to this day.

One of the early Jacobite Rebellions occurred in 1719 when a group of 300 Spaniards landed at Loch Alsh under the tenth Earl Marischal. Joining the Scots Jacobite force, they began to march south but were beaten by government troops in battle at Glenshiel on 10 June 1715 Some folk have claimed to witness ghostly soldiers re-enacting this battle. Other have seen a single spirit, that of a Captain Downes. Some say he was a Dutchman, hence his nickname. of 'An Duitseach', but others claim he was an English officer.

One of the Spanish soldiers killed at Glenshiel is said to haunt nearby Eilean Donan Castle. This spirit is said to frequent one of the bedrooms and carries his head beneath his arm. The castle had been garrisoned by the Earl of Seaforth and fifty Spaniards as a supply base and munitions store. After the battle the Spaniards were imprisoned and eventually sent home to the Iberian peninsula.

A number of Redcoat spirits have been seen on the road up Glen Aray near to Inveraray Castle in Argyll. Marching six abreast, these soldiers are the ghosts of Cumberland's men, who were garrisoned nearby.

The Duke of Argyll, who is chief of the Campbells, had Hanoverian sympathies, so some time in the eighteenth century Inveraray Castle was attacked by a group of Jacobites. Though the nobles had fled the castle a young Irish servant was discovered hiding in the building. He was murdered by the Jacobites and his corpse quartered. Each piece was stuck on top of one of the upright poles of a four-poster-bed in the castle as a warning to the Campbells. The room where the ghost of the boy most commonly appears is known as the MacArthur room, and on some days the bedclothes are mysteriously disturbed, as though someone has slept in the bed, despite the room being locked.

Another phantom scene linked to Inveraray Castle is a boat which sails up Loch Fyne towards the castle and which continues to sail across the land. On it are three men, standing upright. Those who have seen the galley describe it as being very similar to the birlinn, or sailing ship, which appears on the Campbell arms. It is usually only spotted prior to the death of one of the Campbells.

Other ghosts are associated with the seat of the Dukes of Argyll. A harpist is often heard playing in the castle, even when there was no such instrument within the building. The sound of the string music is most often heard in or near the Blue Room, usually only by women, including various Duchesses of Argyll. According to tradition, the harpist is the ghost of a Campbell, captured by Montrose's soldiers in the seventeenth century and hanged in Inveraray.

In the Green Library, and occasionally in other rooms adjoining it, the sound of loud crashing and banging can be heard, as though the furniture and ornaments in the room were being thrown about and smashed. During the inevitable investigations later, nothing is ever noticed missing, nor is there any possible cause for the sounds. In fact, the disturbances at one time became so commonplace that the Dukes and their families just ignored it.

The Jacobite forces were finally defeated at the Battle of Culloden on 16 April 1746. The site of the battle is now protected by the National Trust for Scotland who have a visitors' centre and museum at Old Leanach Cottage. A number of memorials commemorate the clansmen who were killed in action—the Graves of the Clans being but one site. It is there and at the Well of the Dead that most ghostly apparitions have been seen, from single soldiers to complete battle scenes.

It is said that descendants of soldiers who took part in the battle can experience visions of the day should they arrive on the battle's anniversary: An American visitor named Ian MacDonald had such an experience in 1896, when he found himself in the midst of a battle. He was stabbed in the chest and fell from his horse. The American later woke up in hospital where he was told that he had fallen from his horse and had sustained bruises. One person has seen a dead soldier dressed in blood spattered Stewart tartan. Others have seen reflections of soldiers' faces in the waters of the Well of the Dead. It is even said that some folk experience pains in the same parts of their bodies as the wounded spirits.

At nearby Culloden House, which dates back to 1772 and which is now a country-house hotel, the ghost of Bonnie Prince Charlie himself has been seen. Several relics once belonging to the Young Pretender were kept here, including his bed and walking-stick. The house was erected on the site of Culloden Castle, in which the prince spent the night before the battle. Bonnie Prince Charlie's ghost has been seen in various parts of the house, including the library, corridors and bedrooms.

It is perhaps the same ghostly Jacobite army that is said to haunt the byways around Inverness. There are a few accounts of these mounted soldiers appearing at various places around the capital of the Highlands, but they never remain visible long enough for full descriptions to be made. The troops are led by an officer sporting a bonnet decorated with gold braid and a dark blue cloak similar to that worn by the Hussars.

The manifestation of an army which was sent to the Scottish highlands to keep the peace after the battle of Culloden has been seen a number of times at Gairnshiel Lodge in Glen Gairn, near Ballater in Aberdeenshire. The house was formerly a hunting lodge used by Queen Victoria and her family but today operates as a guest house. The army has most often been experienced crossing the old bridge that stands in the hotel grounds at one time the only bridge between Glenshee and Deeside over the River Gairn. I say 'experienced', for as far as I am aware only the sound of the horses' hooves and the cartwheels on the old hump-backed bridge have been heard. This sound, according to locals, is one of the most common paranormal occurrences to take place in the district. Some folk claim that the army comprises a troop of soldiers and their accoutrements under General Wade who was noted for constructing military roads. The bridge across the Gairn was erected by his men in 1750 in connection with a well-known military roadway that leads to Corgarff Castle in Strathdon.

Gairnshiel Lodge itself is said to be haunted by other spirits. A visitor to the glen saw an old woman looking from one of the lodge's first-floor windows. From the description it was reckoned that the woman was the ghost of a former owner of the 'shooting-box'.

Duns Castle is an impressive Gothic building that incorporates an older tower house. Located just outside the village of Duns in Berwickshire, the castle has for many years been owned by the Hay family. The castle ghost appears to be one Alexander Hay, a young son of the family who went to fight in the Napoleonic Wars. Aged only nineteen, he was proud of his uniform and was desperate to fight for his country. He was unlucky enough to be killed in the closing few hours of the last charge at the Battle of Waterloo, on 18 June 1815. His belongings were brought back to Duns, where his uniform and other artifacts are kept in the castle. His spirit also seems to have returned to the castle, for the manifestation of a young soldier has been seen in the Yellow Turret room.

More modern ghosts linked to battles make appearances at Montrose's old aerodrome. This was established just before the First World War to the north of the town on the links. Today the airfield is home to a museum. At least three ghosts appear here, one of them a phantom biplane that had crashed in 1913. This ghost was witnessed on a number of occasions over the years, notably by Sir Peter Masefield in 1963.

The same aeroplane appeared once in 1916, almost causing the death of another pilot. The aerodrome was put on red alert when reports came through that a German aircraft had been spotted.. A fighter aeroplane was scrambled, but despite flying all around the district no sight of the enemy was made. The pilot was ordered to return to base. At Montrose the commander in charge of the air base decided that it was too risky to illuminate the runway fully, so turned on only the lights on the edge of the runway. The pilot was very experienced: so the sparse lighting should have been enough to guide him home. As he descended towards the runway he suddenly pulled up and away from the landing course. Those watching on the ground wondered why he had done so, assuming that he was perhaps just off course. The aeroplane circled the aerodrome once more and started a second descent. Again, just before landing the fighter was jerked off course and the pilot made a quick withdrawal from the descent path. The ground staff could not understand what was amiss, so the commander ordered the whole airfield to be lit up. This time the pilot made a perfect landing and cruised into the parking position.

As he opened the cockpit, the pilot yelled out 'What fool was that who kept cutting me out?' The ground crew replied that there were no other aeroplanes in the air, 'Yes there was: it was some idiot who kept cutting across in front of me' he replied. 'Why do you think I had to keep coming in again?' When he gave a full description of the aircraft it turned out to be a biplane, not unlike a Tiger Moth.

The pilot of the biplane has also manifested his spirit at Montrose. He was Lieutenant Desmond Arthur of No.2 Squadron of the Royal Flying Corps, whose aeroplane crashed here in May 1913. As he was descending from 4,000 feet the starboard wing of his BE2 biplane collapsed and he plummeted to his death. His spirit has been noted on many occasions, Major Cyril Foggin having witnessed it eight times.

The third ghost is that of an RAF flight commander. It is said that he was an unpopular figure and that when his aeroplane crashed here in the summer of 1942 foul play was suspected. The official inquiry cited engine failure as the cause, though many thought that a fitter in the workshops had sabotaged the aircraft during routine maintenance.

A Second World War soldier haunts the Sunlaws House Hotel near Kelso in Roxburghshire. The hotel is owned by the Duke of Roxburghe and forms part of his extensive estate, but it is operated as a top-class hotel. The building dates in part from the fifteenth century, though most of it was refurbished in the late nineteenth century. During the Second World War it was, like many country houses, requisitioned for military use. Sunlaws was converted to an internment centre for prisoners of war and many foreign soldiers passed through its doors. The spirit of a soldier of Italian appearance, has visualized a number of times in the attic rooms of the mansion, and some folk claim that it is the manifestation of a soldier who died of his war wounds. The figure is quite weak in appearance, but from its dress is obviously a soldier.

Some of the hotel staff have also seen the apparition of a woman walking across the entrance foyer of the house. She walks from the bottom of the main staircase toward the lounge and from there into the conservatory. Most sightings have been made in the early hours of the night. No one knows whether the figure was a member of the Innes-Ker family, one of their staff, or someone else.

4

HOUSES AND
HOSTELRIES

It is not only castles and mansions that ghosts seem to frequent. Many accounts exist of strange happenings and unexplained sights in more modest houses, hotels and other such places. Antiquity is by no means the sole criterion for a building to be visited by ghosts, though In many cases the older the place the more likely it is to be haunted.

Edinburgh is surely one of the most haunted cities in Great Britain, if not the world, and a trawl through some celebrated examples will give the reader an idea of the wide variety of ghosts to be encountered.

The Royal Mile is that stretch of the Old Town of Edinburgh which extends down from the castle along the ridge on which the original part of the city was built to the Palace of Holyroodhouse. Both these buildings have ghosts of their own, the former is mentioned in Chapter 3, the latter is noted in Chapter 2. The Royal Mile is made up of five streets: the Castlehill, Lawnmarket, High Street, Canongate and Abbey Stand. Starting from the Castle, we will point out the haunted closes and wynds en route to the Palace. Indeed even a phantom coach and horses has been seen making its way up the Royal Mile. Many old books record sightings of this 'Death Coach', which usually appears before some impending catastrophe.

In the Lawnmarket there was formerly a flat that in the eighteenth century was abandoned by: its owner. According to tradition, the family were serving dinner to a number of guests when something so strange and horrible occurred that they fled from their home. As they did so, they locked the door behind them. After that evening the house was never opened, and all its contents were abandoned to the evil spirits. They even say that a goose in the midst of being roasted was left on the spit. According to Robert Chambers, writing in 1823, No one knows to whom the house belongs; no one ever inquires after it; no one living ever saw the inside of it; it is a condemned house.'

Just off the Royal Mile, down George IV Bridge, we come to Victoria Terrace, scene of the hauntings by Angus Roy, a sailor whose ship was harboured at Leith. Angus had suffered an accident on board his ship in 1820. When he fell from a mast he was left a cripple. He retired to Victoria Terrace where he lived in misery, longing for the sea and hating the children who made fun of his strange walk. After his death in 1840, his spirit returned to torment those who had mocked him. His ghost is still apparently seen dragging its leg as it makes its way along the terrace.

The West Bow is the short road joining Victoria Street with the Grassmarket. In the seventeenth century this was the home of Major Thomas Weir, who became one of the most talked-about citizens in the city, and his house was celebrated as the most haunted house in Britain.

In life Major Weir was regarded as one of the city's most upstanding residents. Probably born in Lanarkshire, he took part in the struggle against the Roman Catholics in Ireland in 1641. He remained a bachelor all his life, living with his sister, Grizel Weir. On the surface he was an honest, pious and decent man, yet in 1670, aged seventy, he suddenly confessed to hundreds of crimes including witchcraft. At first no one in the city would believe such an apparently upright character. Yet he persisted in his accounts of fraternizing with the Devil, and implicated his sister in the process. Many folk then began to assume he was mad, but his confessions continued. Doctors were called to examine him and they all agreed that he was perfectly sane.

Major Weir was tried for his crimes on 9 April 1670 and the court decided that he was guilty of the acts to which he had confessed. Both he and his sister were executed the major being strangled and burned midway between the city and the port of Leith, Grizel hanged in the Grassmarket. In the fire the major's stick, which many believed had special powers, jumped about and took longer to burn than was normal. At Grizel's execution she tried to remove all her clothes, so that she could die 'with all the shame she could'.

The house in which the major lived remained empty for a hundred years or so after his execution. Reports of supernatural activity began to filter through, however. Some folk claimed to have seen a dark coach and horses pull up at the front door, supposedly sent by the Devil in order to transport Major Weir and his sister to hell. On some nights at midnight the house was seen to be brightly. It, yet everyone knew that it was empty. Sounds of dancing and screeching emanated from within as well as the whirr of a spinning-wheel. Major Weir's sister had been a weaver in her earthly life. Others claimed to have seen the major emerge from a close next to the house, mounted on a dark headless horse, on which he would gallop up the street amid flames.

In the middle half of the eighteenth century the house was leased by an old couple, Mr and Mrs William Patullo, who were attracted by the extremely low rent. During their first night staying there, they were woken by a ghostly calf that crossed the room and leapt on to their bed. After staring at them for a while, it turned away and slowly vanished. The next day the Patullos fled and the house lay empty again. Its condition gradually worsened until in 1830 it was demolished and a new building was erected on the site. Sir Walter Scott also wrote about the haunted house:

> Bold was the urchin from the High School who dared approach the gloomy ruin at the risk of seeing the Major's enchanted staff parading through the old apartments, or hearing the hum of the necromancer's wheel, which procured for his sister such a character as a spinner.

At the head of the High Street stands the great church building of St Giles; though often called a cathedral, it is more correctly the High Kirk of Edinburgh. It did act as a cathedral, however, from 1633 to 1638 and from 1661 to 1689 when Kings Charles I and II tried to impose Episcopacy on the Scots. Surrounding it on the south side is Parliament Square, where stands Parliament House and the High Court. This was formerly the kirkyard of St Giles; the grave of the reformer John Knox is marked by his initials. Within the square stands the Mercat. Cross, location for a ghost story that some say was in fact an elaborate hoax, performed at the request of Queen Margaret in order to try and prevent King James IV marching to England and his death on the field of Flodden in 1513.

Originally the Mercat Cross was the spot where proclamations were read out to the inhabitants of the city. In August 1513 a city merchant, Richard Lawson, was passing by early one deserted morning. He was startled to see at the cross the figure of a ghostly herald. The manifestation lifted his scroll and from it began to read a list of all the men who were to die on the battlefield. The list started with King James IV and the herald read out hundreds of names in descending order of rank: dukes, earls, viscounts, lords, knights and gentlemen. Lawson was unable to move as he listened to the many names, but when he heard the herald call out 'Richard Lawson, merchant in Edinburgh', he fell to his knees and began to pray, asking for the Lord to have mercy on his soul.

Come September Lawson had either forgotten the herald, or else was a very brave man, for he joined the Scots forces on their march to assist France in their fight against the English. Some 35,000 Scots followed the king southwards and after a few days met on a field at Branxton, in Northumberland. The Earl of Surrey led the English forces to victory, killing 10,000 Scots, including the king, fifteen earls, seventy lords and numerous knights. The only person not to die whose name had been read out at the Mercat Cross was Richard Lawson. He returned safely to Edinburgh, where he often recounted the tale. It was eventually heard by Robert Lindsay of Pitscottie (c. 1532–80), a noted historian of the day, who recorded the tale in his *Historie and Chronicles of Scotland* hence its long survival.

Sir Walter Scott recounts the tale of a ghost of one of the city's guardsmen. He states that the man was a Highlander who joined the town guard. Grey-haired and greybearded, he is sometimes seen walking round the statue of Charles II in Parliament Square, carrying a Lochaber axe over his shoulder.

Almost across the High Street from Parliament Square stands the City Chambers. These were erected in 1753 as an Exchange, from plans drawn up by john and Robert Adam. A tenement building collapsed in 1751, providing a convenient city-centre site for the building. Part of the chambers is built above one of the old lanes of the city, Mary King's Close. This was partially destroyed by fire in 1750, hence its incorporation in to the new Exchange buildings. Not all of the close was demolished before the new building was erected. Being constructed down the slope of the hillside, only the upper floors were removed, the lower walls conveniently providing foundations for the new structure. The old close was shut off and forgotten about for many years: it was used only by engineers who had to check over the services for the chambers, it having been a convenient place to lay cables, pipes and ducts.

Mary King's Close was the part of the city that suffered most during the outbreak of plague in 1645. It is reckoned that a higher proportion of people died in that area than anywhere else in Edinburgh. It was finally decreed by the councillors that the close should be sealed off to stop the disease from spreading. These orders were acted upon, and for many years the lane remained empty. After a while, however, the population of the city began to grow and more housing was badly required. Some folk felt that the close should be reopened and the houses reoccupied.

Thomas Coltheart was one of the first to take his family into one of the old houses. They were just getting settled in when the flickering flame of a candle burning in the room turned a bluish colour, making the atmosphere suddenly sinister. Then they saw a severed head with a hoary grey beard pass along in mid air and as time passed this was joined by an arm holding a lamp. Next there appeared two or three pairs of feet, skipping across the floor as though partaking in a dance. They also saw a headless dog and cat. At first the family thought that they were just imagining these visions, but as the days passed other residents in the close began to report strange yet similar sightings. After a week or so the occupants were so terrified that they fled their homes. Mary King's Close was sealed off once again and remained so until the fire of 1750. Coltheart's accounts were published in *Satan's Invisible World Discovered* in 1685.

Other accounts have circulated of ghostly experiences within Mary King's Close. A retired soldier and his family occupied a house in the close and were disturbed by the sight of headless animals and a young child. There are also those who say that the scratching sounds heard behind one of the walls are made by a chimney-sweep who died whilst cleaning out one of 'Auld Reekie's' flues. It is possible to look up the close from a gate in Cockburn Street, and guided tours of the lane are available.

Further down the Royal Mile, just at the top of the Canongate, stands Chessel's Court, an old tenement building of 1750 which has been restored and still provides accommodation. In the latter half of the nineteenth century the upper flat was occupied by an old lady named Mrs Gordon. She and a number of the residents had a feeling that the building was haunted, for they often experienced breathing sounds and weird sensations. Each time they tried to investigate the area from which the sounds seemed to emanate they stopped. Although they had never seen a ghost, they suspected that the cause of their disturbances was probably a woman who used to live in the court and who had hanged herself there. Finally Mrs Gordon's brother saw the spirit, a tall woman dressed in black silk, her skirt fully distended with layers of crinoline petticoats. When he described to his sister what he had seen she confirmed that the ghost was indeed that of the hanged woman. Her brother refused to visit Chessel's Court again.

In the same area a tale is told of a young girl, the daughter of a distinguished family who had a town house hereabouts in the eighteenth century. It was discovered that the girl was pregnant out of wedlock and, what was worse, that the father was a servant lad. The girl was forbidden to leave the house again, for fear of the shame which she would bring on the family. The minister was called and was asked to perform the last rites for the girl but he was a bit suspicious for he felt that the girl was healthy enough. The family told him that she was suffering from an incurable disease and that she had not long to live. On beginning the prayers of preparation for death, he heard the sound of a baby crying in another room. The family realized that his suspicions were roused still further and so told him not to ask any questions if he valued his life. As he left the house, they thrust some money into his hands.

Later in the same day word reached the minister that a house in the Canongate had caught fire and that a young woman had been killed. The minister rushed up the street to see if he could be of any assistance, but was shocked to discover that the blazing house was the one he had visited earlier. He was afraid to say anything in case of reprisals. Years later, before his death, the minister revealed what had happened that day, and that he thought the fire was arson, a means of killing the girl and her lovechild.

The house in the Canongate was rebuilt and occupied for many years thereafter in peace. But in the second half of the eighteenth century the building again caught fire. On that day the apparition of the girl appeared and yelled, 'Burned once, burned twice, the third time I'll scare you all' The ghost has not been seen since.

In the Old Town lived a butcher whose wife had died at an early age. After giving her a decent burial the flesher found himself a new girlfriend—within four days of the funeral! He was at her house in Provost's Close one evening, lying in her arms on the couch. After a particularly amorous kiss, the butcher looked up at the widow of the sitting room and there saw the face of his late wife. He got such a shock that he fled the house and could not face the girlfriend for a while after afterwards. A few days later he made his way back to the girl s house, but the spirit of the woman returned to the window, her grave-clothes wrapped around her body. The butcher was so frightened that he never visited the girl again. Soon after, he caught some disease from which he failed to recover and died.

Another Old Town house that was haunted was the one belonging to William Ruthven, first Earl of Gowrie. After his execution in 1584, his ghost was reportedly seen standing at the doorway, dressed in the garb he wore on his last day. This building has long since been demolished, but folk still claim that his phantom haunts the Immediate locality.

The New Town of Edinburgh was laid out on ground to the north of the Nor' Loch, now Princes Street Gardens, in 1767. There are a number of hauntings located within these houses and buildings.

The General Post Office in Waterloo Place, on the corner with North Bridge, was built in 1861. It occupied the site of the old Theatre Royal and the appropriately named Shakespeare Square. The Theatre Royal was built in 1768 and for many years plays and recitals were produced with great success there. However, ghost actors seem to have had a habit of returning after the curtain had gone down at night and re-enacting performances during the hours of darkness: The spirits were overheard by the stage manager and his family, who lived in the flat above the theatre. When the playhouse was closed in May 1859 a booklet detailing the history of the building alluded to this haunting.

The West End of Princes Street is said to be haunted by a young woman who spends her time crying in sorrow. According to the tale, handed down over the years, she was the wife of a man murdered somewhere at this end of the street. When she found the spot where his death had taken place she was so overcome with grief that she stumbled in front of a horse and carriage. The horses reared up in fright and trampled her body. The carriage wheel then rolled over her killing her outright.

The ghost of the woman, named Moira Blair, has appeared a number of times in the street, usually in the evening. One man spotted her crying at the corner with Hope Street. At first he assumed it was a mortal person, but she did not answer him when he asked what was wrong. Walking off, he was astonished to see the apparition gradually fade away into nothing. Other folk claim that sobbing sounds heard in the kirk of St John at the west end of Princes Street Gardens emanate from this ghost.

India Street extends northwards from Queen Street Gardens towards St Stephens. The houses date from soon after 1807 when the ground was offered for feuing. Number 56 probably dates from the 1820s, and was built in the Georgian style. The house is inhabited by a ghost that seems fond of company, for its presence is usually felt when a party or similar social gathering is taking place. There have been no distinct sightings of the spectre, and thus no one is sure whether it is male or female; 'shadowy' or 'transparent' is how it is usually described. It is most commonly seen in the hall, progressing at a few feet above floor level. Many notable people have witnessed the strange shadows, including Sir Iain Moncreiffe of that Ilk, Lady Compton Mackenzie and Brodrick Haldane.

Regent Terrace is a smart line of houses built along the slopes of Calton Hill in 1825 following the design of William Playfair. In 1979 four students living in a flat here experienced many weird noises, from children crying to deep breathing, yet they were sure that the house was empty. On several occasions small items such as watches and jewellery would disappear for days on end, only to turn up elsewhere. The flat also seemed to be haunted by an invisible cat that would jump on to beds whilst people were sleeping in them. The earthly cat that lived in the flat was often too scared to enter certain rooms, in particular the kitchen. The students eventually found the flat too frightening to live in, and moved elsewhere.

At Edinburgh's west end is Rothesay Place, erected in the 1870s and 1880s. Strange happenings in a house here began to take place when the tenant took possession of an old piece of wood that had once been in the cottage of a friend who lived in the north of Scotland. Soon after the piece of wood was installed the occurrences began: doors would open and close, drawers would slide out of the chest, objects fell from shelves and at times the noxious odour of a pipe tainted the air. All these goings-on were blamed on a ghost called 'Merry Jack Tar', a sailor who had once lived in the cottage from where the wood had come. The ghost is said to have haunted the house in Rothesay Place for many years, but things seem to have calmed down now.

Across the Dean Bridge in Queensferry Road stands the Learmonth Hotel, part of a terrace that dates from 1873 onwards. The hotel is home to a poltergeist that likes to play tricks on the guests and porters. Several times doors have opened or closed by themselves, and have even managed to unlock themselves shortly after the key has been turned. Guests have found tea-makers and hair-driers inexplicably switching themselves on. The same spirit seems to enjoy whistling, as can be deduced from the strains wafting up empty corridors.

In nearby Ann Street, which dates from the early nineteenth century, number 12 was for many years haunted by a former resident, Mr Swan, who had been sent to sea in his youth. He died whilst abroad, but his spirit returned to Edinburgh where it remained for many years, appearing in this house to a number of people. A local minister was called to perform an exorcism. This seems to have worked for a while, but in 1936 the house was sold, and for some unknown reason this triggered the reappearance of Mr Swan. His presence was seen by many, especially the young children who slept in one of the bedrooms. They often reported that a small man dressed in black often came in to say goodnight to them.

Also at the west end of the city is the district of Dalry, once frequented by a popular ghost named 'Johnny One Arm'. His manifestation was seen several times, always distinguishable by the fact that his right hand was missing. 'Johnny One Arm' was in fact John Chiesly, who was executed in 1689. He had shot the Lord President of the Court of Session, Sir George Lockhart of Carnwath, outside the Old Bank Close in the Lawnmarket. Lockhart had awarded Chiesly's wife a large annual payment in settlement of their divorce. Chiesly was quickly apprehended and tortured to find out if he had any accomplices. Finally he was hanged at the city gallows, but the hand which pulled the trigger was cut off beforehand.

The corpse of Chiesly was stolen from the gallows one night. No one knew who did it; certainly it was not his wife. The mystery of the missing body remained unsolved for almost three centuries until 1965, when an old house was being rebuilt in Dairy Park. When the tradesmen prised up the hearth stones the skeleton of a man was discovered, minus its right hand. Johnny's mortal remains were buried elsewhere, and his spirit has not been seen since.

To the south of Edinburgh's Old Town at Bruntsfield stands the Boroughmuir annexe of James Gillespie's School. This was erected on the site of an ancient mansion known as Wrychtishousis, or Wrightshouses. In the middle part of the eighteenth century the house was home to a General Robertson, who lived there whilst his Perthshire house at Lawers was being altered. He took his black manservant, 'Black Tom', with him, but during his first night there the valet was disturbed by the spirit of a decapitated woman and a young child. They appeared during the night wandering back and forth across the room. The next few nights saw the return of the ghosts, and the servant asked to be given a different room in which to sleep. General Robertson was not a believer in spirits and dismissed Tom's accounts as rubbish. The servant was greatly relieved when work at Lawers was complete and he could return to his home.

After a gap of some years, and after the death of General Robertson, a member of the family that owned Wrychtishousis visited Lawers. She repeated a tale that probably accounts for the ghosts in Bruntsfield. It seems that many years earlier the house was lived in by James Clerk, his wife and child. He had been given the property by his father in 1664. Clerk had gone abroad to fight in some war but died in battle. When word reached home of his death, his younger brother killed the wife and child so that he would inherit the estate. He disposed of the corpses in a chest, but the woman's body was too big to fit in. The only option was to cut off her head. The chest was placed in a small closet and the door sealed off. The Merchant Company later acquired Wrychhshousis for development purposes. When the house was being demolished the locked closet was discovered. The chest was opened to reveal its grisly secret, as well as a note of confession left by the brother.

On the western fringe of Edinburgh is the district of Corstorphine, at one time a separate village in its own right. In Dovecote Road stands an old dovecote originally part of the now-demolished Corstorphine Castle. This area is haunted by a White Lady that has been seen wandering around the old grounds. She is thought to be Christian Nimmo, who fell in love with James Baillie-Forrester, second Lord Forrester of Corstorphine Castle. She was the niece of his first wife, Joanna Forrester. James and Christian were in the habit of meeting in secret beneath an old sycamore tree, but sometimes their trysts resulted in arguments, for James could not control his love of drink. At one meeting the arguments over James's alcohol problem became so heated that Christian drew out Forrester's sword and killed him in a frenzy.

Christian was quickly arrested and confessed. She petitioned the Privy Council to admonish her, claiming that she carried Forrester's child, but was turned down. She escaped from prison dressed as a man, but was recaptured on Fala Moor, south of the city, and was executed on 12 November 1679. Her spirit has remained at Corstorphine ever since, wandering among the houses that were built in the grounds of the old castle. Some say that she carries with her the sword used to kill James, and some say that there is a curse on the dovecote: whoever pulls it down will die. The old sycamore still grows at the east end of Dovecote Road, protected by a Preservation Order and the Corstorphine Trust.

Across Scotland are numerous pubs and hotels that are reputedly haunted, and not only after visitors have been sampling their wares! In my home town of Cumnock in Ayrshire stands the Craighead Inn, an old pub that was probably erected in 1722, when

The Craighead Inn, Cumnock, Ayrshire, dates from 1722 and is said to be haunted in the attic rooms.

a lease was drawn up requiring an annual rent of £21 plus two hens and two loads of coal. The building stands two storeys plus an attic high, and it is one of the attic rooms that is said to be haunted. A number of weird sensations have been experienced over the years and for a time no one would stay there overnight. In the 1970s the landlord threw down a challenge to anyone to sleep the night in the room, and this was successfully achieved. The room has since been modernized and the spirit no longer appears.

Also in Ayrshire is the famous Turnberry Hotel, overlooking the two championship golf courses and the mountains of Arran across the Firth of Clyde. The hotel was built in 1904 by the Marquis of Ailsa in partnership with the Glasgow and South Western Railway Company, but has been extended a number of times since. During the Second World War the hotel was requisitioned for use as a hospital. The present staff wing was used as a medical centre, which included an operating theatre. It is in this wing that inexplicable sounds have been heard—sounds reminiscent of an older hospital. Trolleys rattling along the corridor floor and knocking against swing doors have been heard, but nothing is ever seen. Some folk also claim to have smelled disinfectant, but on investigation could find no source for the odour.

Heading over the Galloway Highlands from Turnberry, we come to Dumfries, largest town in the far south of the country. There were two haunted hotels in the burgh, the King's Arms and The County, but both no longer operate as such.

The King's Arms Hotel stood near the junction of the High Street with English Street.

The Post Horn Inn at Crawford, Lanarkshire, was said to be one of the most haunted buildings in Scotland.

The ghost here was a Grey Lady, believed from her apparel to be of Victorian vintage. The ghost appeared as a young woman in her twenties and was seen on and off for over a century. Her most common haunting location was the lounge, where she was even noted watching the television!

The County Hotel was demolished in the early 1980s, having stood at the foot of the High Street. It was formerly known as the Commercial Inn and before that as the Blue Bell Inn, and during the Jacobite uprising was visited by Prince Charles Edward Stewart. The soldiers under the Bonnie Prince stopped off at Dumfries on their march to and from Derby, and on the return journey demanded £2,000 and 1,000 pairs of shoes from the inhabitants. For some reason the spirit of Bonnie Prince Charlie kept returning to the town, and usually appeared in the County Hotel, where a lounge was named in his honour. It was in that room that the Prince held court in the town.

Due north of Dumfriesshire is the county of Lanarkshire, which roughly covers the same area as the river basin of the upper Clyde. There seems to be nothing but haunted inns in this county, the first one we come to being in the village of Crawford. Now bypassed by the M74, the village was at one time an important resting-place on the great road from Glasgow to London. In the village stands the old Post Horn Inn, one of the change-houses on the route. This inn boasts three ghosts indeed, when the inn was put on the market in 1994 it was described as Scotland's most haunted house, though there are many other claimants to this title.

The inn was erected in 1744 and was much frequented over the centuries. The present dining-room was at one time the stables and here can be found the ghost of a young girl, aged nine or ten years old. According to legend the girl was the daughter of a former innkeeper and his wife who was accidentally killed when a coach and horses knocked her over in the Main Street. The girl had liked horses—hence her appearance in the old stables, where she skips up and down, singing to herself.

There is also the tale of a ghostly figure who appears less regularly than the young girl. He was one of the coachmen who were driving a carriage up the valley towards the Beattock Summit in February 1805. It was snowing, and as they neared the top the snow lay so thickly that they were unable to follow the road. At one point they careered into a ditch and their coach overturned. The two men set out for help, but one of them died of exposure within a few miles of the accident. The other actually reached Crawford, but by this time the storm was so wild that he missed the old Post Horn by a short distance and also succumbed to the elements. One of the recent owners of the inn was at the bar one stormy night when he saw a figure in a dark cloak pass the window. He went out to speak to him, but was amazed to find no one in sight, nor were there any footprints visible in the fresh snow.

The third ghost is thought to be that of another young girl, this time around five years of age. She was supposedly hanged in the nearby 'Hanging Wood' for stealing a loaf of bread. The ghost of this girl is not restricted to the inn, and in fact is more commonly seen among the hills that surround the village.

From Crawford the Clyde meanders sedately through its dale before changing pace considerably, plunging over falls and cataracts in the gorge below Lanark. In the county town's Bloomgate stands the Clydesdale Hotel, built in the second half of the eighteenth century on the site of a Franciscan friary founded by King Robert the Bruce between 1325 and 1329. It is claimed that the beer cellars of the hotel were at one time part of the crypt of the monastery. Here the ghost of a monk is sometimes seen, but more commonly felt or heard. When the hotel staff are in the cellars they often report feeling the spectre passing by them. Sounds are often heard within the cellars, from rattling glasses to slamming doors.

On the Carluke road, just outside Lanark, stands the Cartland Bridge Hotel, at one time a country house (known as Baronald) then a nursing home. An impressive baronial building of 1890, it was erected for a Mrs Paris but passed into the hands of the Farie family, who retained it for many years. The house is frequented by two ghosts, one a Blue Lady, the other a young girl. The Blue Lady has not been identified, but the manifestation takes the form of an aged lady who wanders around the building. The young girl is believed to be Annie Farie, daughter of the family who owned Baronald. She was killed in a riding accident at the age of seven. Her ghost often appears in a room that at one time was her nursery and she can be identified from a surviving portrait.

Farther down Clydesdale we come to the town of Larkhall. On the west edge of the town, by the side of the Millheugh Bridge which crosses the Avon Water, stands the Applebank Inn, an old public house dating from the early eighteenth century. The inn is haunted by a ghost that really belongs to Broomhill House; but when that mansion was demolished the lintel over the doorway was relocated at the inn—hence the, ghost's adoption of Applebank.

According to tradition, Broomhill House was owned by Captain Henry Montgomery MacNeil, after whom MacNeil Street in Larkhall was named. MacNeil was a seaman, who travelled the world, trading in many distant countries. He made his fortune and retired to Millheugh, bringing with him an Indian woman whom some say was his wife, others that she was merely a servant. After a period of cohabitation, Captain MacNeil began to tire of the cultural differences between them. At length she disappeared from Broomhill. Some say she was murdered by the Captain. Others say he threw her out of the house and she died whilst roaming the countryside. At any rate, the ghost of a Black Lady returned to Broomhill, where her figure was often seen looking from the windows. The spirit has also been recorded in nearby Morgan Glen and in the orchards and gardens which adorn Clydeside.

When the Captain died and Broomhill gradually fell into ruin, the lintel was taken to Applebank where an extension was being erected. It took five men to carry the huge block of stone to the building site, but sometime during the night the stone was thrown from the new walls into the middle of the road. Naturally, the Black Lady was blamed for this deed. Over the years the ghost has also moved articles around the inn, set tables and hidden objects.

In the 1960s the television journalist Fyfe Robertson brought his camera crew to Applebank Inn where he hoped to perform a live exorcism on the *Tonight* programme. At first the camera lenses froze over, despite the clement weather. The filming went ahead, but the director was killed in a car crash within a few days. Some say it was the Black Lady's revenge.

East from Lanarkshire is the county of Peebles. The county town has two hotels boasting ghosts, and the village of West Linton has a former inn that is haunted. Medwyn House stands up the Lyne Water valley from the village centre, located amid trees. It was built in the fifteenth century as a coaching inn on the road from Edinburgh to Lanark, the old coach road originally running past the house, and closely following the even older Roman Road. The building has been much extended and altered since that time to create a country house. The vicinity of the house is haunted by a coach and horses that often passes by. Guests at Medwyn House have heard the sound of horses' hooves and the ringing of the coachman's bell.

The Cross Keys Hotel in Peebles' Northgate is reputedly haunted by the first landlady to run the hostelry, she having taken over from her father. Marion Ritchie (died 8 February 1822) was the original of Meg Dods of the Cleikum Inn in Sir Walter Scott's novel *St Ronan's Well*.

The ghost of Marion Ritchie likes to move items from place to place, to switch electrical equipment on and off and to break glasses. She materializes in various places, including the former stables, which are now a restaurant; however, the proprietors, who have many experiences of her, claim that Bedroom 3 is the most haunted room in the hotel. It was in this room in September 1975 that a group of parapsychologists, armed with tape recorders, awaited the spirit's appearance. The sound of Miss Ritchie „Vas heard and captured on tape, or at least so they thought: when the tape was played back later it sounded like a cartoon character's voice. The second time the tape was played the voice sounded much fainter and the third time it had disappeared altogether. On another occasion one of the hotel's chefs tried to take a photograph of the spectre, but as he was focusing his camera an unnatural force pushed him backwards down the stairs causing him to break his leg.

The County Hotel, which is located in the High Street, has a dining-room that the proprietors find difficult to heat. There are also inexplicable occurrences in the hotel,

Cross Keys Inn, Peebles, where the first landlady, Marion Ritchie, still keeps an eye on the customers.

like items moving or disappearing for a while, and on odd occasions an incorporeal female voice tan just be made out in the kitchen. The proprietor tried to find out from the locals some historical basis for the hotel's supernatural happenings but was unable to do so. It was not until 1989 that a visitor from America pieced together the background to the hauntings.

Jack Priestley was the grandson of a Peebles woman, and he recalled a story passed on by her in his childhood in the early 1900s, he being eighty-one years old in 1989. It seems that there was a maid working in the County Hotel in the first half of the nineteenth century. The hotel was being altered at the time, and a tunnel behind the dining-room was opened up. The maid entered out of curiosity but she slipped and fell, and was trapped there overnight. When the tradesmen arrived the next day they found the girl's cold and lifeless body. She was buried in the local St Andrew's kirkyard. From that day onward the spirit of the girl was often noted in the building, sometimes seen, but mostly making its presence felt by moving objects and whispering quietly in the kitchen.

Due south of Peebles, across the Manor Hills, we arrive at St Mary's Loch, much beloved by Sir Walter Scott, James Hogg and other literary figures of the nineteenth, century. They often met at a hostelry which still exists, known as Tibbie Shiel's Inn from the woman who established it. Her proper name was Elizabeth Shiel, and she married a mole-catcher named Robert Richardson. When he died at an early age in 1823 leaving his widow with six children, Tibbie opened her cottage as an alehouse. Its popularity

The former County Hotel, Dumfries, where the spirit of Bonnie Prince Charlie is said to have appeared on a number of occasions.

grew, folk admiring the surrounding country-side and enjoying the fireside conversation. Tibbie died on 23 July 1878 aged ninety-six and was buried in Ettrick kirkyard, where her headstone can still be seen.

The ghost of Tibbie Shiel still frequents this romantic spot, though she is rarely seen. Normally the feeling of a cold hand on your shoulder as you sit merrily drinking in the bar is enough to indicate her presence. Some say that this is Tibbie forcing her way through to the fireside, as she was wont to do when the inn was busy. Many people have experienced this, and turned round to find no one there. Another unexplained happening involved a poker, lying by the fireside, which was mysteriously catapulted across the room.

Tibbie Shiel's Inn is also haunted by the spirit of a dog that has been noticed in the bar. According to the local folk this apparition is the pet of the proprietor at around the turn of the twentieth century. Then an old man, he was still fit enough to keep the place ticking over. One day he travelled to Selkirk on business, leaving his dog tied up in the bar. The innkeeper died whilst he was away, and the dog starved to death before he was found.

The Royal Hotel in Cupar in Fife was erected around 1835 in the Doric style. The site was previously a burial ground associated with a monastery, which explains the monk that still frequents the site. He is most often seen in one of the hotel's large function rooms. The hotel has also witnessed a little poltergeist activity over the years.

In Perth's South Street stands the Salutation Hotel, one of the oldest hotels in the country. A plaque commemorates the visit of Bonnie Prince Charlie, and his spirit still seems to haunt the hotel. In 1975 Jack Mott awoke in his bedroom to witness a figure, dressed in a green tartan, standing at the door. For some reason Mr Mott was not perturbed by the vision and went back to sleep. He awoke later on in the night, and saw the same figure again, but as he stared at the apparition it gradually faded away.

Bridge of Earn is located a few miles south of Perth. The Moncreiffe Arms has a long reputation as a haunted inn and many guests have reported hearing strange noises coming from the upstairs rooms. These include the sound of footsteps on bare floorboards (which are actually carpeted) and crying (when no one is in the inn). In recent years the landlord went to use the bathroom but found the door locked. This he thought strange, for he knew he was the only person in the building. Behind the door he could hear the sound of splashing water, as though someone was taking a bath. He assumed one of the guests must have returned unexpectedly and turned to walk away. But when he looked back over his shoulder, he discovered that the door was now open. On entering the bathroom, he found that the bath and all the towels were still perfectly dry.

Jumping across to the west coast of Scotland, we find some more haunted hostelries. The most southerly of these is the Coylet Inn, which stands beneath Beinn Ruadh on the shores of Loch Eck, eight miles from Dunoon. A Blue Boy frequents the inn, roaming through the rooms in search of his mother. He also has a habit of shifting objects around, so that items left in one room mysteriously vanish and reappear in another. Staff at the inn have encountered wet footprints in the upstairs hallway, yet there are none on the stairs leading to it.

According to the tale, the young boy stayed at the inn a number of years ago with his parents. He was prone to walking in his sleep, and one night at the Coylet he wandered from the inn outside. He meandered in slumber across the road towards Loch Eck, where he was drowned. When his corpse was found the next day it was blue from cold. Since that night guest and drinkers at the inn have experienced his spirit from time to time.

The story of the Blue Boy was used in a film of that name made in 1994 for television by the director Paul Murton. He came across the story whilst making another film at Loch Eck. His camera scanned the loch and took in the Coylet Inn, but when the movie was being edited a bluish mist appeared on the film that had not been visible at the time. Neither the director nor the cameraman could work out the cause of the mist. It was not until they spoke to the landlord of the Coylet that he told them the story of the Blue Boy. Perhaps his spirit had been captured on film...

North from Argyll, passing up the Great Glen, or Glen More, we arrive at Loch Ness. On the western banks, three miles from Invermoriston, stands Alltsaigh House. Previously the Alltsaigh Hotel and tearoom, and then the Loch Ness Youth Hostel, erected sometime in the 1930s, the site was originally occupied by an old inn or change-house, which had a haunted room within it. Here a ghost by the name of Annie Fraser has been said to appear. Many folk over the years have heard phantom footsteps in this particular room when it was ostensibly empty. Others have witnessed the girl pacing through the woods up the glen of the Allt Saigh. According to legend, Annie Fraser was being courted by two brothers, Alasdair and Malcolm MacDonnell, but neither one knew of the other's association with the girl. One evening, in the gloaming, Alasdair met Annie and they took a walk up through the birchwoods by the side of the Allt Saigh. They climbed the hillside and came to Loch a' Bhealaich, where they settled down in the grass. Unknown to the pair, they were followed by Malcolm, who, when he saw them embrace, confronted them and challenged his brother to a fight. In the ensuing mêlée a knife was drawn and one of the brothers was killed. The survivor turned on Annie and thrust the knife into her chest for good measure, killing her instantly. He dragged her body back down the steep slopes of Creag Dhearg to Alltsaigh, where he buried her below the floor of what was to become the haunted room. History records that this brother was later drowned in Loch Ness as he sailed over towards Foyers.

Much farther north, on the west coast of Sutherland, is the Kylesku Hotel, located at the southern end of the Kylesku Bridge. For years the hotel was an ideal watering-hole for those waiting to be transported across Loch a' Chairn Bhain on the ferry. Indeed, the building was originally known as the Ferryhouse, but it has been much extended and modernized since that time. In. the eighteenth century a local fisherman found a barrel of whisky, lost from a ship that sank in the Minch, and dragged it back to the Ferryhouse. He heaved it up to the loft of the house, access to which was reached by an external stairway, a common feature of old buildings. He invited a few friends to share his good fortune, but as the night wore on their spirits got out of control and they began to quarrel. At length the fisherman's son tried to break up the party, for it was almost the Sabbath, but a scrap broke out and the boy ended up by pushing his father down the stairs, breaking his neck. In agony, just before expiring the fisherman yelled out that he would get his revenge on the boy.

It so happened that within a few months the son was out fishing and fell overboard into high seas. His corpse was washed up on the shores of Loch Glencoul. The spirit of his father still returns to the Ferryhouse, usually on the anniversary of his death.

Over on the east side of the Grampian Mountains, at Ballater in Aberdeenshire, can be found the Pannanich Wells Hotel. Located in South Deeside road, the hotel dates from 1760 and grew in popularity when 'taking of the waters' was a common means of curing ailments. The building is haunted by a Grey Lady who has been seen by numerous people. This spirit circulates both inside the inn and outside in the grounds as far as an old oak tree. At other times only the sound of the ghost is heard, or else the noise of moving furniture and opening doors.

There is a wide selection of small houses, spanning the country, that are reputed to be haunted. Not all of them are old, for that matter. Taking another journey round the country, we will note haunted houses as we go. We have mentioned Edinburgh's haunted houses at the beginning of this chapter, so we will set off from there.

Across the Firth of Forth from the capital is the kingdom of Fife, home to a number of ghosts. In the twin towns of Anstruther stands Johnstone Lodge, located at the top of Kirk Wynd. (We say 'twin towns' because there are two distinct communities, Easter and Wester, in separate parishes either side of the Dreel Burn.) Johnstone Lodge is in Anstruther Easter, a largish town house built in 1829 following the design of architect George Smith. The owner, George Dairsie, was a merchant seaman. On his travels round the world he fell for a Tahitian girl who was to become his wife. She was Princess Tetuane Marama, daughter of the king of Haapiti, one of the Pacific islands. Unfortunately, when Princess Tetuane moved to Anstruther at her husband's side, she found she could not settle in Scotland, for the weather was far colder than in her native islands. She longed to return home, but stayed faithfully by her husband's side. At length she died and was buried in the town's kirkyard, where a memorial tablet of 1898 commemorates her. This is located on the south wall of the kirk and contains the longest word used in an epitaph in Britain, if not Europe. The word, which is her full name, is 'Tetuanireiaiteraiatea'.

After the funeral service the ghost of a woman that resembled the princess began to haunt Johnstone Lodge. She appeared in a number of rooms, as well as on the balcony over one of the building's bay windows. Johnstone Lodge was acquired by the National Trust for Scotland and converted into flats, from which time the ghost of the Princess has rarely, if ever, been seen.

Before the Tay bridges were built one had to journey inland from Fife to Perth before heading further north, unless one was lucky enough to catch a small ferry. We will follow the old route, for in Perth are another two hauntings we must take account of. One of these takes place in a house known as Belfield. The 2nd/1st Highland Artillery Brigade was stationed in Perth in the winter of 1915. The men were billeted at a school in the town, the officers at Belfield, which was about half a mile out of town. One night as they settled down to sleep, the officers were disturbed by knocking at the windows. When they got up to peer out there was no one there. Returning to bed, the men heard the noise again, yet still no person was visible. Getting annoyed, the men arranged to sit up in front of the widows and wait till the banging started again. On hearing the sound, the men drew up the blinds quickly, revealing a face at the window. The figure turned on its heel and made its way across the lawn. Some of the soldiers ran out into the grounds but could see no one again. When they looked outside the window where the figure had appeared they discovered that there were no footprints in the snow. There was little sleeping that night, and the next day many of them requested that they be allowed to join the junior soldiers at the school.

The second ghost associated with the Fair City dates back to 1838 and seems to have made a solitary appearance. According to the old story a woman named Anne Simpson was living in Perth near to the poverty line. She got into debt, having run up three shillings and sixpence on the slate with a grocer in the town. A spirit began to appear to Anne in the guise of a washerwoman. So terrified was she that Anne finally visited the local priest to ask him if he could solve her problem. The priest was able to end the regular hauntings, but not by exorcism. Instead he paid off Anne's grocer's bill and the ghost appeared no more!

Many hillwalkers claim that a number of the bothies they use for overnight stops are haunted, and tales abound of the supernatural in these remote cottages. Perhaps the best-known haunted bothy is Benalder Cottage, located near the southern end of Loch Ericht, deep in the heart of the Grampian Highlands. Many folk claim to have experienced something unnatural here, though I must admit that when I stayed overnight in it there were no signs of any unearthly spirits.

The climber Robert Grieve, later Sir Robert, stayed in the cottage with friends shortly after it was abandoned by the shepherd in 1949. They were sitting in one of the downstairs rooms enjoying a post-prandial smoke when they heard the sound of heavy footsteps in the other downstairs room. They opened the door and went through to speak to the visitor but found the room empty. Puzzled, they thought the person must have left again, and so went to bed. Yet the sound returned, this time outside. Robert Grieve and his friend searched the bothy and its surroundings but found no one. Back in their sleeping-bags they heard the noise again, this time accompanied by the sound of furniture moving in the next room. A third search failed to reveal any possible source for the noises.

Other folk have heard similar sounds at Benalder over the years, since the cottage was turned into a bothy. On one occasion in 1970 the climber and poet Sydney Scroggie was staying in the cottage with a friend. Lying in their sleeping-bags on the floor, they heard the sound of heavy footsteps in the room next door, but on checking found the room empty. They knew it should be, for anyone going into it would have had to pass by them in any case. Tucked up once more in their sleeping bags the men were astounded to see an unopened box of biscuits they had placed on the mantelpiece fly across the room and hit the opposite wall before dropping to the ground. There was no natural explanation for how this could have happened, and when the box was opened not one biscuit was found to have been broken.

As the two men were pondering on a possible solution for the mystery, the door burst open suddenly and a heavy thud caused the floorboards to vibrate. No one had come through the door, nor was there enough wind to have blown the door open.

The door at Benalder, which has figured in a number of supernatural happenings, is very difficult to open the first time one arrives at the bothy. Climbers arriving at the cottage have to really force the door to get it to open, even though it is not jammed Second and subsequent openings find the door swinging ajar quite easily.

According to many folk, the last full-time resident at Benalder was a stalker, who hanged himself behind the front door: the ghost is supposed to be his earthbound spirit. However, history tells a different story, for the last permanent residents in the cottage were Mr and Mrs McCook, the husband having died at Newtonmore in 1951. According to relatives of the family, there were no unnatural occurrences recorded at Benalder during the McCook's tenancy, so any ghost which haunts the bothy must have arrived after they had gone.

Another tale of ghosts in bothies is set in the Galloway Hills. A group of hillwalkers were intent on reroofing the old shepherd's cottage of Black Laggan, near to Loch Dee. They had drawn up their plans and were about to start work when they began to sense that the place was haunted. In fact, so unnerving was the atmosphere at Black Laggan that they gave up their task and restored the ruinous cottage at White Laggan, just half a mile away.

The old manse at Lairg in Sutherland stands in ruins. In 1826 two girls were playing in the dining-room when they heard a knock at the door. On answering it, they found a very old and thin man, dressed in a long dark robe and a dog collar. He looked into the manse and seemed to peer closely round the room before turning away. The girls ran upstairs to tell the minister that there was an old preacher looking for him. When he came to the door the old minister had gone, and there was no sign of him in the vicinity, despite the whole countryside being visible around the manse. The girls told the minister what the man had looked like, and from their description he recognized the likeness of the Revd Thomas Mackay, who had died twenty-one years earlier, before either of the two girls was born.

More recently, and long after it had become a ruin, the manse at Lairg also seems to have frightened off two poachers, who had hidden their equipment there. From the weird sounds and cold atmosphere within the building the poachers fled homewards, leaving their fishing gear behind.

Another northerly manse is that at Durness, on the north coast of Sutherland. It is said to be haunted by the spirit of a death herald. Many years ago the minister was regularly disturbed by the sound of knocking at the front door. He invited an associate minister from Kinlochbervie to the manse and when the knocks were heard again sent him to answer the door. On pulling the door ajar, the visitor saw before him the figure of an old man covered in graveclothes. He got such a fright that he sped back to Kinlochbervie on his horse. Within a month he had died at the early age of forty-six. His wife, who was a few years his junior, died shortly afterwards.

At Port Ellen on the island of Islay is a country hotel that was created from the conversion of an old distillery. It is said to be haunted by a burglar, who once forced his way into the distillery, where he found malt whisky barrels in store awaiting maturation. The intruder imbibed so much of the golden liquor that he became drunk and on trying to escape left by way of an upstairs window, forgetting he was not on the ground floor. Killed by the fall, he is said to haunt the spot to this day, though the window from which he plummeted was bricked up after the distillery and the hotel were extended.

There are two farmhouses between Kilmarnock and Mauchline in Ayrshire inhabited by ghosts. Both are named Bargower, as the main steading is spelled; the nearby cottage is styled Little Bargour. Bargower is haunted by the ghost of a former tenant, John Neill Drummond, who died in 1938. A later occupant of the farmhouse, Mrs Sadie Caldwell, awoke in the middle of the night to see the apparition of the farmer standing at the foot of her bed. He was dressed in the old-fashioned night attire of a farmer of his period—a long-sleeved semmit and long johns. Mrs Caldwell states that she was not scared by the ghost's presence; indeed, she said that she just turned round and fell sleep again. At a later time she met the farmer's second son and checked with him whether his father looked like his elder brother. The answer was yes. The phantom farmer has appeared a number of times to the Caldwell's children, Mairi, Billy and Ian.

Mrs Caldwell also recounted to me the story of when new owners moved in to Little Bargour. After a time the woman of the house asked her if there had ever been a lame person living in the cottage, for they could hear the sound of a person walking around the attic. The occupants found out that there had indeed been a crippled girl resident in the cottage, two owners back. The later proprietors had never met these folk, yet knew that one of them had a limp from the sound of the footsteps.

We have already noted Lanark's ghostly monk in the Clydesdale Hotel. The town is also home to a ghostly nun, resident in the council offices. The building was at one time used as a hospital, but became offices after the medical practice was transferred to a new building in the 1960s. The site occupied by the hospital had been used as such since at least the fifteenth century, and was formerly run by nuns. There have been several sightings of a ghost wearing a nun's habit in the building, most commonly in, the evening when the building is quiet.

The village of New Lanark was established in the eighteenth century as a community for workers employed in the mills. David Dale, the founder, carried out a number of reforms in the village, making sure that the large number of children employed in the mills were properly educated and fed. After many years of neglect, the buildings of New Lanark have been restored and today form a major tourist attraction in Clydesdale. The village is the haunt of a number of ghosts. One female phantom appears in the house located over the village shop, at one time the doctor's surgery. Mary Graham who used to live in this flat at the turn of the century, recalled her paranormal experience for an archive of oral material preserved in the village.

I was by myself in the back bedroom. I had a bed to myself. I wakened frozen. I just wakened frozen... it was a coldness that just seemed to freeze me. When I opened my eyes the figure was coming towards me. I thought I'd shut my eyes but I did get a glimpse of her.

She had an old-fashioned Inverness cloak and a wee black hat, but she had a veil over her face. I didn't see her face. I froze. I couldn't move. It was terrible. When I did open my eyes she put out her hand to me, I remember that. She had gloves on. That was when I opened my eyes and I saw her. She had turned away from me. The next thing I saw there was a bright red spark going through the door. That was all I saw. The door was bolted and nailed—we never used it.

Mary told her story to her parents, and they confirmed that the house was supposed to be haunted, but that the ghost would not harm her. In her old age she discovered that her younger brother, Alan Graham, had also seen the ghost, but because of his age his parents had persuaded him that It was a dream. He believed this to be the case, and did not discover the truth until late in life. Both accounts tell a similar tale, their descriptions of the ghost's dress match. The woman's identity has not been ascertained, but it has been suggested that she may have died in the surgery.

Just outside the town of Peebles, which we have already visited in this chapter, grow three large trees, standing in a straight line. They are located in a field off Craigerne Lane, a road that heads south out of the town, circling Cademuir Hill and arriving at Kirkton Manor. On a number of occasions a phantom human figure has been seen at the middle tree. This usually occurs at around nine o'clock in the evening. Sometimes an eerie light precedes the appearance of the ghost. Who the figure is or was is not known.

To the east of the village of Walkerburn, eleven miles down the River Tweed from Peebles, stands Holylee House. On the estate is the cottage of Gatehopeknowe, which was the home of the gamekeeper at the beginning of the twentieth century. One day his son was cleaning a shotgun when it went off, killing him instantly and splattering parts of his body against the ceiling. The ghost of the boy continues to return to the cottage, and is often seen looking out from one of the windows. Residents are often unable to sleep because of the uneasy feelings that they experience whilst staying there.

On the edge of the Lammermuir Hills in East Lothian is the village of Innerwick, a tiny place with a parish church, five miles from Dunbar. At the beginning of the eighteenth century the local minister was a Revd Ogilvie, and though he never told anyone of his meeting with a ghost, he recorded his experiences in a diary which was found after his death. On 3 February 1722 he was returning home to his manse after having paid a social call to a nearby farm. As he walked along the rural lane he was stopped by a ghost riding a horse. The figure, dressed from head to foot in black, bellowed to him, 'I am Maxwell, Laird of Coul, and I have a job for you.' The minister was so shocked that he could not speak. The spirit then disappeared. Revd Ogilvie became convinced that the spirit would not appear again, for over seven weeks passed without a sign. On the next occasion the ghost did not utter a word, despite the minister asking him what he wanted. The ghost appeared to the minister a third time and at last spoke to him. He said that during his life he had swindled one of his relatives out of money, and he now wished to make amends. The minister, however, did not want any part of his scheme. The spirit appeared a fourth time to the minister but the repeated refusal to help must have deterred him, for he never appeared again.

It is not only old properties that are liable to have ghosts: there are several modern houses known to be haunted. Some of these are council-built houses erected since the last war.

In Cumnock in Ayrshire a former council house in the street known as Riverview is haunted. This house was erected in 1960 in the estate known as Barshare, winner of a Saltire Society Award. The building was used as a police house, but one day a constable who had been posted there committed suicide while on duty. From that time on the house was difficult to let because of the restless spirit that dwelt there. A minister was asked to exorcize the house, which he did, but still the house could not be let. At length the house was sold off and the ghost of the policeman seems to have found his peace.

In the New Town of Livingston in West Lothian a couple from Glasgow were living in a modern flat. Over a spell of time they found mysterious hand and finger-prints on the walls of their home, and it is said that on one occasion the spirit carved its initials on the wall above their bed as they slept. The couple actually saw the ghost, a spirit dressed in white, often sitting in their armchairs. It was also known to have passed through doors. Eventually the couple relinquished their tenancy in 1971.

At Kilsyth in Stirlingshire another householder has tried to have a ghost laid to rest by calling on a priest to bless her home. Patricia Canavan lived in a council house at Kirklands Crescent, which is nearby an old graveyard. Soon after moving into the house in September 1992 the hauntings commenced and her young son related the appearance of an old man in his room each night. The spirit of a young boy has also been seen, and the family dog refuses to enter the boy's bedroom.

At Greenock in Renfrewshire a priest exorcized a council flat in November 1991. Michelle Kane had experienced many unearthly sounds in her home; from scratching at the windows to creaking floorboards. One room was always cold despite the central heating being turned up full. Her daughter saw a hairy beast with horns fighting with an old man in her bedroom. Eventually the council had the Kanes rehoused and after the exorcism the spirits have not returned.

At Liberton in Edinburgh a council home in Hazeldean Terrace is said to be haunted by the spirit of a soldier who fought at the Battle of Prestonpans in 1745. He was taken prisoner but died en route to the gaol in the city centre.

In Fife two cases of haunted council houses are recorded. In Cowdenbeath a young couple were allocated a house in Greenbank Drive, but shortly after taking the keys discovered that the building had a ghost. This spirit caused some major thuds in the couple's bedroom. They described its appearance as not unlike Robert Burns, but surrounded by a warm glow. Finally in 1970 they had to move from this house to escape the continual disruption.

In Kirkcaldy in November 1972 a family of seven experienced an unnatural phenomenon, one that made them leave their beds in the middle of the night and run out into the street. All seven of them experienced the weird sensations at the same time in the terraced house, and none was keen to return. The atmosphere in their home, had suddenly turned cold and damp, as though a soaking wet blanket had been thrown over them.

A council house at Lochgilphead in Argyll was the spot chosen by a ghost to try and choke the residents.. In. 1990 Christine Brown was woken in her sleep to find invisible hands trying to strangle her, as well as a great weight resting on her chest. Terrified, she tried sleeping in different rooms, but still the invisible spirit managed to reach her. The local minister, Revd John Callen, was called to bless the house, after which the hauntings ceased.

A private house in Ayr's Belmont Road was haunted by an old woman dressed in black with a white apron. In September 1982 Maitland and Heather Hunter purchased the house and began to settle in. One day Heather was working in the kitchen and suddenly became aware of the old woman's presence. She had her back to her, and seemed to be preparing food on a worktop. It was someone she had never seen before, and after a short while the apparition disappeared. Shortly after, the same thing happened. Mrs Hunter said that she felt no fear, and has not seen the ghost since. No one else in her family has witnessed the ghost, but it is thought to be the earthbound spirit of the previous owner, an older woman, and that she just wanted to investigate the new owners of her house.

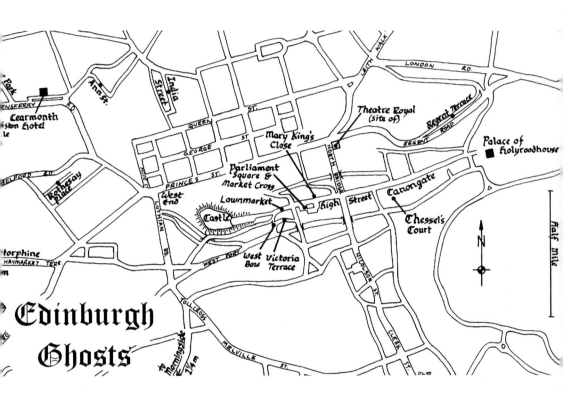

5

HAUNTED CASTLES

Scotland is a land of castles. Hundreds of them are dotted all over the country, and there are hundreds more that over the centuries have long, since crumbled away to nothing. Many of the surviving castles and tower houses are still occupied, some are preserved as places of historic importance, and there are numerous abandoned ruins. It seems that every one has a tale of the supernatural associated with it, though many are just local stories told by elders to entertain young boys. A good number of the castles, however, are inhabited by well-documented ghosts, having been seen time and again by different people.

Let us take a journey around these haunted sites, starting in Glasgow, then heading north. Between Chryston and Moodiesburn, on the road to Cumbernauld, stands Bedlay Castle, most of which dates from the sixteenth century, but which has incorporated a twelfth-century structure. It was at one time used as the palace of the bishops of Glasgow. Here, around the year 1350, Bishop Cameron was discovered dead, his corpse lying face down in a small loch. The castle has been haunted by his spirit ever since. In the 1880s the local priest had to be brought to exorcize the castle, the disturbances having become too disruptive for the owners to bear. The exorcism does not seem to have worked fully, for as recently as the 1970s, when the castle was occupied by an antiques dealer and his family, the ghost was still active. The dealer's children saw what they described as a 'big man' in their room, and the sound of feet have been heard pacing across rooms.

Continuing north from the city we soon reach upland countryside, the Kilpatrick and Campsie hills providing a delightful skyline to the metropolis. If we cross the Campsie Hills from the Clachan of Campsie by way of Muir Toll we reach the village of Fintry, located in the county of Sterling. To the north of the village stands Culcreuch Castle, a fifteenth-century tower house and ancestral seat of the Clan Galbraith. Still the Centre of a 1,600-acre estate, the castle has been converted to a fine country-house hotel. One of the rooms in the original keep half of the castle is haunted, although most accounts describe the ghost as 'amiable'. The ghost's identity is unknown, but it is said that a murder was committed in this room in 1582. The ghost is fond of playing a clarsach or Celtic harp, and the sound of music is sometimes heard elsewhere in the building. The haunted room at Culcreuch is better known as the Chinese Bird Room, from the wallpaper which dates from 1723. During my stay at the castle I slept next door, in the Keep Room, but no music was heard nor strange spirit seen.

A Dutch guest at the castle was a keen researcher on matters paranormal. At night, before retiring to bed, he set up his camera on a tripod and when darkness filled the room he opened the shutter. Next morning he closed it again before the lights were turned on. When he returned to the Netherlands and had the film developed, he discovered that as well as his sleeping figure, the camera had captured a figure seated on the kist at the foot of the bed. It was dressed in white clothing, but there were no other clues as to who the person was.

Eerie bagpipe music has also been heard in the dining-room at Culcreuch. The noise seems to come from the room below, but despite a thorough search of the whole castle no source for the sound can be found. The then owner of the castle, Hercules Robinson, recorded the music and sent a tape to a music society in Edinburgh. He was amazed to discover from them that the sound was made by bagpipes with no drones, a feature which was added to them as far back as Jacobite times, in the middle of the eighteenth century.

Taymouth Castle stands at the foot of Loch Tay, a vast gothic pile of around 1800, built for the fourth Earl of Breadalbane, created first Marquis In 1831. The building is haunted by a ghost that seems to appear just before some tragedy is about to befall a Campbell family member. It is rarely seen, but it has appeared in an alcove within the castle. Several people have heard its footsteps clumping around the large building. One of the housekeepers at Taymouth remembers hearing the phantom footsteps during the First World War. She was alone in the library, the Breadalbanes being elsewhere. The sound of the feet came through an open door, then slowly quietened as the ghost walked down the corridor. Her search to see if anyone was there proved fruitless.

The castle was used in recent years for conferences and training courses. Some students attending these courses were so frightened by their ghostly experience that they refused to stay in the castle. Indeed, things got so bad that the castle's principal gave his staff instructions to make no mention of the ghost.

Another Campbell seat is Cawdor Castle, home to the Earl of Cawdor, and a Campbell stronghold since 1511, when the lands were acquired from the Calder, or Cawdor, family through a forced marriage. The castle, which is situated six miles from Nairn, is bedevilled by unnatural changes in temperature and disappearing objects. One room in particular remains cool all year round. The most noted apparition at Cawdor, however, is the ghost of a young woman with no hands.

According to stories handed down the generations, the girl was daughter of one of the early Earls of Cawdor. The first Earl had his title created in 1827. The girl, who was slim and attractive, fell in love with the son of a neighbouring chieftain. However, this chieftain's family were enemies of the Campbells and the two lovers had to meet in secret. One day Lord Cawdor came across them cuddling in the woods. Vowing that they would never embrace again, he hacked off his daughter's hands.

A similar tale of forbidden love accounts for the ghost at nearby Castle Grant. An old structure that has been much rebuilt over the years, Castle Grant stands above Grantown of Spey, twenty-two miles south-east of Nairn. It was for centuries the seat of the Grant, then Ogilvie-Grant, families, but is no longer part of their extensive estates. The ghost at Castle Grant is usually seen in one of the bedrooms of the original tower, sometimes known as 'Barbie's Tower'. This room is generally referred to as the Haunted Room.

Some folk claim the ghost was one Barbara Grant, daughter of the head of the family in the sixteenth century. She fell in love with a lad from the nearby village, a boy of inferior rank, according to her father. The latter had made arrangements for her to marry someone more suitable, but Barbara could not abide him. As a punishment her father locked her away in the small dry closet located just off the bedroom. Her father

Culcreuch Castle, Stirlingshire, where the ghostly sound of bagpipe and harp playing has been heard in some rooms.

Cawdor Castle, Nairnshire, has a spirit of a young girl with no hands.

Brodick Castle, Island of Arran, where the Grey Lady is thought to be the ghost of a woman killed by the plague.

hoped that a few days of imprisonment would change her mind. Instead, however, the girl's resolve grew stronger, and she refused to submit to her father's plans. The father left her locked up for a few weeks more, till at length the girl died. Her spirit has been seen in the Haunted Room, flitting from one side to another. Part of the way across she stops to wash her hands, then disappears through the doorway leading to the spiral staircase.

We have already met a number of Green Ladies in Scottish castles and country mansions, but there are other colour variants, too. Aldourie Castle is basically a neo-baronial mansion of 1853 added to a tower house of the seventeenth century. It stands on the east shore of Loch Ness. A Grey Lady frequents the oldest part of the castle, though her identity is not known. The Grey Lady takes a walk from a bedroom at the west end of the castle through the building to the main sitting-room.

Another Grey Lady haunts Brodick Castle, the largest castle on the Island of Arran and now in the care of the National Trust for Scotland. Part of the building is very old, having been erected in the thirteenth century. The castle has been extended several times since, however, most notable being James Gillespie Graham's west wing of 1844. The Grey Lady has most often been seen on the back stairs. One person followed the spirit from here along the hall to the servants' quarters, where she disappeared.

Various theories have circulated about the ghost's original identity. Some folk say that she was one of three women who arrived at the castle suffering from the plague around 1700. They were locked up in the castle dungeons and died there. Why only one

Neidpath Castle, Peeblesshire, has the spirit of a White Lady who died pining for her lost love.

of the three haunts the building is itself a mystery. Indeed it may lend more weight to a rival theory. It is said that in the seventeenth century there was a maid in the castle who committed; suicide. This may explain why the Grey Lady makes her way to the servants' quarters.

At one time there was a housekeeper in the castle named Mrs Munsey who claimed to have some form of psychic ability. She claimed to be able to talk to the dead using a form of automatic writing, and carried out an experiment to find out more about the Grey Lady. From this it was claimed that the girl had been in service in the house at the same time as Cromwellian soldiers were occupying the castle. She is supposed to have had an affair with the commander of the troops and become pregnant by him. Rather than lose her job and be stigmatized, she committed suicide by the shore.

There are another two ghosts associated with Brodick. The first is seen within the castle, the second within the grounds. In the castle library the figure of a man has been noted, wearing a long green jacket and breeches and usually seated in a chair.

The third ghost of Brodick is the famous White Deer, which only appears when the chief of the Hamilton family is about to die. The deer herald has been noted a number of times in recent years, and its appearance has in fact tied in with a death of one of the main chieftains of the Hamiltons.

To find a White Lady we will journey to Neidpath Castle, a mile or so out of Peebles. The tower stands virtually entire, apart from one corner, which was destroyed in an attack by Cromwell's forces in 1650. Still owned by the Earl of Wemyss and March, the

Craignethan Castle, Lanarkshire, has a White Lady ghost which appears to have no head and whom some think is the spirit of Mary Queen of Scots.

castle is open to the public throughout the summer months. The White Lady's original being is not known, but some claim that she was the Maid of Neidpath, by which name the ghost is also known.

The story of the maid was versified by Sir Walter Scott. It seems that the daughter of the Earl of March fell in love with a local laird's son. Though he was heir to a small estate, Lord March felt that his daughter was worthy of better things, and tried to find a titled gentleman for her to marry. The original lover decided to emigrate, to try and make his fortune. The girl remained at Neidpath, crying incessantly and pining for her lost love. Her health worsened and she was in grave danger of dying. After a time the laird's son returned to Tweeddale. Lord March realized that his daughter would marry no other, so he had her bed carried to a balcony from which he knew she would be able to obtain a view of the lad as he travelled through the glen, and in this way, he hoped, her health would bloom again. However, the boy passed by Neidpath and because of the girl's condition did not recognize her. Despite her waving, he did not acknowledge her presence and she died of a broken heart.

The White Lady is rarely seen at Neidpath, yet the castle exudes an unnatural atmosphere. One visitor arrived at the castle, walking through the main doorway. So terrible did she immediately feel that she ran back out and could not be persuaded to re-enter. On other occasions doors have been noted opening and closing by themselves.

Craignethan Castle, which stands on a rock bluff overlooking the Nethan Water, above Crossford in Clydesdale, has a White Lady ghost. Maintained by Historic Scotland, the

Claypotts Castle, Dundee, is the home of a
White Lady as well as a brownie, the latter
carrying out chores on behalf of the owners.

castle was a seat of the Hamilton family. The spirit of a headless lady dressed in white
has been seen, though infrequently, in the old tower at the castle. Some say that the ghost
is of Mary Queen of Scots, who was beheaded in 1587. She did not stay at Craignethan,
but is known to have passed through on occasion.

Other even fainter spirits haunt Craignethan, too. Some dogs, which are more
receptive to things we cannot feel, will not cross the bridge over the moat from the outer
courtyard to the inner one. In the custodian's cottage, which is built into the castle wall
and which dates from 1661, female voices have been heard, but not clearly enough to
make out the words. Two young boys saw a mist appear from a castle wall, drift across
one of the rooms and disappear.

At Sanquhar in Dumfriesshire stands the ruins of Sanquhar Castle, ancient seat of the
Crichtons. The ghostly White Lady which is sometimes seen here is thought to be the
spirit of Marion of Dalpeddar, who disappeared in 1590 without trace. No one knew
where she had gone, but it was said that Lord Sanquhar was somehow responsible. In
1875 when excavations were being made in the castle, the skeleton of a young woman
was found lying face down within a pit and disinterred. The White Lady appears to
have long blonde hair, and the skeleton seems to confirm the link, for traces of golden-
coloured hair were found with it. A rare visitor, the White Lady's appearance is said to
trigger trouble for the Crichtons.

A second ghost haunts the castle of Sanquhar, one who makes his presence known
by the sound of groans and rattling chains. The invisible ghost is that of John Wilson,
who was falsely accused of certain crimes by the sixth Lord Sanquhar. According to the
Records of the Privy Council, Wilson 'was a trew man, nevir spotted nor suspect of any
sic crymes as he [Lord Sanquhar] falsli objectit against him'. Wilson was hanged on the
Gallows Knowe, and his spirit has haunted Crichton's castle ever since.

Within Dundee's suburbs stands the delightfully attractive tower-house known as Claypotts Castle. Erected by Gilbert Strachan in the late sixteenth century, the castle was for many years supposedly the haunt of a brownie, who would perform many chores on behalf of the household. It was supposed to have been frightened away by one of the female servants who refused to allow it to help. Claypotts is also the home of a White Lady that appears on 29 May each year. The ghost is said to be that of Marion Ogilvy, a lover of Cardinal David Beaton, who was murdered on that day in 1546.

The White Lady of Dunrobin Castle in Sutherland haunts the uppermost room in the ancient tower that lies at the heart of this great nineteenth-century fantasy castle. Margaret, daughter of the fourteenth Earl of Sutherland (he died in 1703), fell in love with Jamie Gunn, groom on her father's estate. When her father discovered the romance he was so angry that he fired Gunn and expelled him from the estate. His daughter was locked up in the old tower. Gunn and Margaret were still very much in love, and plans were somehow made for the girl's escape. A length of rope was smuggled to her prison, and she made her way across the castle's battlements. Word leaked out that Margaret was making a getaway, and the earl and his steward set out in chase. When Margaret spotted her pursuers, she threw herself to death from the castle walls. Her crying spirit still haunts the room that had been her prison, a room which has since become disused.

Glamis Castle is noted for its many ghosts, among them a White and a Grey Lady. Standing by the village of Glamis in Angus, the castle is the seat of the Earl of Strathmore and Kinghorne, the Queen Mother being Elizabeth Bowes-Lyon, daughter of the fourteenth Earl. Princess Margaret, sister of Queen Elizabeth, was born here. According to one tradition, the Bowes-Lyon family cannot see ghosts.

The Grey Lady is the spirit most often seen at the castle, or more specifically in the chapel, although she has also been witnessed in the crocktower. The chapel is one of the most unusual rooms in the castle, the ceiling being totally covered with paintings, and the walls plastered with portraits of Christ, saints and biblical scenes. The late Lady Granville, sister of the Queen Mother and wife of the fourth Earl Granville, spotted the Grey Lady seated on a pew in the chapel. She has been seen a couple of times by the previous Lord Strathmore.

It is thought that the Grey Lady is the ghost of Lady Glamis, widow of John, sixth Lord Glamis. She remarried, to a Campbell of Skipness, but remained at Glamis where she brought up her sons, the Lord Lyon and Gillespie Campbell. The sixteenth century was a time of witch-hunting and Lady Glamis was tried for witchcraft at the command of King James V, though he was probably more keen to have her killed for her membership of the too powerful Douglas clan, having been born Janet Douglas, sister of the Earl of Angus. The castle was besieged in order to capture her, her second husband, her son and an old priest for supposedly having plotted to poison the king. Campbell of Skipness, Lady Glamis and her eldest son, Lord Glamis, were taken prisoner. The boy was given a reprieve, but was kept prisoner until James V died. It later turned out that the accuser, William Lyon, who was a distant relative, admitted to fabricating the charges. Lord Glamis was released and in 1543 was restored to his honours, forfeited estates and ransacked castle. He died in 1558.

Lady Glamis was tried as a witch and on 3 December 1540 burned alive at Edinburgh Castle. She was taken from her cell there and tied to a stake on the Castle Hill. After tar and oils were poured over her she was set alight. Her husband and son were forced to watch from the castle. On the following day Campbell tried to escape from the castle but fell to his death on the rocks because his rope was too short. The spirit of Lady Glamis is said to appear when a tragedy is about to occur in the Bowes-Lyon family.

The White Lady is less often seen, but there are accounts of her on the same day at the same time from three independent witnesses.

One butler formerly working at Glamis apparently hanged himself in a room in the castle, since known as the Hangman's Chamber. His spirit still haunts this room.

Just inside the room known as the Queen Mother's sitting-room, next to the door, there is a stone bench where the spirit of a youthful black boy has from time to time been seen. His identity is unknown—perhaps he was a page in service—but he seems to be waiting patiently for something to happen or someone to appear.

In the early history of Glamis many members of the Ogilvy clan were murdered within the castle. According to the ancient story, the Ogilvys were at feud with the Lindsays, an inter-familial battle that had lasted for many years. One day the Lindsays chased the Ogilvys southwards across Strathmore. The Ogilvys arrived at Glamis, where they pleaded with Lord Glamis to protect them. He let them in to the castle, and persuaded them to hide in a secret room. However, once they were hidden Lord Glamis locked the door and left them there. The clansmen starved to death, screaming out in hunger. Many folk claim that the screams of these men can still be heard at times throughout the castle. Less probable, however, is the claim that one of the later Lord Strathmores opened a room that had been locked for years only to faint on finding it full of skeletons!

In the attractive grounds of Glamis, in that part known as the Angle's Park, there appears a spirit that seems to flit across the grass. He most often materializes on nights when the moon is quite full and because of his speed is known as Jack the Runner.

Tales exist of other lesser known ghosts at Glamis, including the Tongueless Woman. According to tradition, she witnessed some evil deed and to prevent her telling the authorities the perpetrators of the crime cut out her tongue. There is also the ghost of a tall man dressed in a heavy overcoat buttoned right to the neck and that of an armour-clad soldier.

One of the more famous spirits to haunt Glamis is that of Earl Beardie, or Earl Patie as he is sometimes known. It is reckoned that he may have been the first Lord Glamis, who died in 1459. Born Patrick Lyon, he was held in England as a hostage for the ransom of King James I from 1424 until 1427. He was created Lord Glamis in 1445. He was a compulsive gambler and many tales recount how he would spend days on end competing against others at cards and dice. The stories also accuse him of gambling with the Devil himself (probably because of his habit of playing cards on the Sabbath), the game having taken place at Glamis late one night. 'Earl Beardie', as he was known from his impressive whiskers, apparently died very soon after this event.

According to a Victorian story, there was born to Patrick, third Earl of Strathmore, a son who was badly deformed, misshapen, and covered with a mass of hair. As he was the first-born son in the family he was due to inherit the titles and estates, but the story goes that the family had him locked away in a secret chamber in the huge castle. There he was kept hidden from the outside world, and a younger son was proclaimed Lord Glamis and heir. When the deformed son died is not known (if he ever existed), but there are folk who claim that he lived until as recently as 1921.

Folk who visited Glamis added fuel to the fire of speculation by relating that they were woken during the night by the sound of grunts and other strange noises. Some even claimed to have been disturbed in their beds by the feeling of a hairy body against their faces. It is said that a tradesman working in Glamis discovered the disfigured Earl at one time, and was promised a large sum of money to assist his emigration to Australia on condition that he would keep his mouth closed. The room in which the deformed Earl was imprisoned is not known, but the walk around the castle battlements where he was allowed to exercise, is known as the Mad Earl's Walk.

The secret of the Glamis heir is said to be known only to the Earl, his heir and the estate factor. Should the heir to the title be in his youth, the secret is kept until he comes of age. It is told in some circles that often a happy-go-lucky heir suddenly turns solemn and inward-looking when he is told the truth about the beast. When someone asked the thirteenth Earl (who died in 1904) what the secret was, he is said to have answered, 'If you could guess the nature of this secret, you would bend down on your knees and pray to God in thanks that it is not yours'.

Understandably, there have been many attempts to find out the true secret of Glamis over the years. Sir Lyon Playfair, Lord Playfair (1818–98), a distant relative of the Lyon family, wrote in his autobiography, 'I naturally did my best to discover the famous secret and the awful mystery connected with it. I drew my own conclusions, which were probably as erroneous as those which have been made by others in regard to this famous secret.'

Sir Walter Scott visited Glamis to experience the unnatural atmosphere of the place for himself. In his diary he noted: 'It left me petrified. I must own that when the door was shut I began to consider myself as too far from the living and somewhat too near the dead.' He did not experience any ghosts, though. He also stated that 'a feature of Glamis is a curious monument to feudal times, being a secret chamber, the entrance of which, by the law or custom of the family, must only be known to three persons at once, namely, the Earl of Strathmore, his heir apparent, and any third person whom they take into their confidence.'

The account of the starving of the Ogilvys recalls the tale associated with Balcomie Castle in Fife. Built in the latter half of the sixteenth century, the tower stands near to Fife Ness, a few miles from Crail. It is said that around the time of construction a young boy was heard whistling by a general and for this was punished by being locked up and starved for a while. However, he died before being let go, and from that time onward the castle is said to have been haunted by the youth. His ghost is not seen, but the sound of whistling is heard in the five-storey keep.

A tale of starving is also linked with Spedlins Tower in Dumfriesshire. An old legend recounts how Sir Alexander Jardine took a local miller named 'Dunty' Porteous prisoner, Jardine having the right of pit and gallows because he owned the feudal barony. Porteous was placed in the castle's pit, a windowless chamber measuring 7½ by 2½ by 11½ feet deep, the only means of entry being through a trapdoor in the ceiling. Jardine then travelled to Edinburgh with the key of the trapdoor in his pocket, forgetting all about Porteous. In a severely starved condition, the prisoner chewed his hands and feet but eventually died of hunger.

The ghost of Porteous haunted Spedlins for many years thereafter, though it is said that it was finally laid to rest 'by means of a black-lettered Bible'. In *The Antiquities of Scotland* by Francis Grose, published in 1789–91, he states that 'The castle was terribly haunted till a chaplain of the family exorcized and confined the bogle to a pit, whence it would never come out, so long as a large Bible, which he had used on that business, remained in the castle.' It is said that when the Bible was sent to Edinburgh to be rebound in 1710 the ghost reappeared, threatening the laird and his wife. The castle was

Hermitage Castle, Roxburghshire, where the spirit of Sir Alexander Ramsay has appeared a number of times.

a ruin for many years, but has been restored and reoccupied. The Bible has remained in the possession of the present chief of the Jardines, Sir Alexander Maule Jardine. Many boys in Annandale used to recount that if you put a stick through the keyhole of the door of Spedlins Tower, when you pulled it back through, the bark had been chewed off by 'Dunty' Porteous.

Another Border castle has a ghost that once died as a result of starvation. Twenty-five miles east of Spedlins, on the moors above Newcastleton in Roxburghshire, stands the noble pile of Hermitage Castle, built in 1244 by Walter Comyn, but much altered since that time, and now protected by Historic Scotland. In 1342 Sir Alexander Ramsay of Dalhousie was captured by Sir William Douglas and held prisoner here, eventually starving to death. It is said that a few grams of corn fell into the dungeon from the granary above, prolonging Ramsay's death by seventeen days. His apparition has been seen wandering around the ruins.

Hermitage was visited for a few hours in 1566 by Mary Queen of Scots when she visited the Earl of Bothwell. Her journey left her with a fever, for she lay in bed at Jedburgh for ten days thereafter. This is just one place where her apparition has been seen, usually dressed in white.

A third ghost associated with Hermitage, Lord Soulis, lived here for a time, gaining

Drumlanrig Castle, Dumfriesshire, is one of a select number of haunted places where the apparition is of an animal, a monkey in this case.

the epithet 'Bad Lord Soulis' from his habit of practising sorcery. He is said to have murdered many people in his lifetime, from young children to adults, having used their blood in his magic potions. At length Lord Soulis's misdeeds were discovered and a group of men captured him. He was covered in a sheet of lead and his body boiled in a cauldron at the stone circle known as the Nine Stanes. History, however, tells us a different tale, for it is recorded that Soulis died in prison at Dumbarton Castle.

Hermitage was placed in care by its owner, the Duke of Buccleuch and Queensberry. The Duke still owns Drumlanrig Castle, a magnificent red sandstone mansion standing in Nithsdale. Here three ghosts—two female figures and an ape-like animal—have been sighted.

One of the female ghosts, said to be the spirit of Lady Anne Douglas, has been seen moving around the castle carrying her head in her hands. The second woman is much younger, and always appears wearing a long, flowing dress. It is said that she only appears to folk who are ill.

The most unusual ghost is undoubtedly the 'monkey': It can be seen in an apartment of the castle known since at least 1700 as the Yellow Monkey Room or Haunted Room. There is no known record of any monkeys ever having been kept in the castle as pets or as part of a menagerie. In any case, not all accounts exactly tally: some describe the phantom as just a 'furry creature'. Among the many witnesses of this ghost is Princess Alice, Duchess of Gloucester, who as Alice Montagu-Douglas-Scott was brought up at Drumlanrig.

Spectral monkeys or apes are rare, but there are a few known dog or hound ghosts. One of the most significant hauntings took place at Inchdrewer Castle, near Banff, though the witnesses did not at first realize that the dog they had seen was a spirit.

The celebrated Scots author Nigel Tranter was visiting Inchdrewer as a guest of the owner in charge of restoration work, Robin Mirrlees, Count de la Lanne. Tranter and his wife were taken to the castle by the contractor, who had the only other key, Mirrlees being absent in London. When the door was unlocked and opened they were surprised to encounter a large white dog—a chow or samoy—walking out of the castle and bounding across the fields. The builder was horrified, for the castle door had been locked for more than a week and he reckoned that the dog must have been locked in all that time. On entering he expected the castle to be in a terrible state but there were no traces or smells of a dog to be found. Further research unearthed the fact that Inchdrewer was traditionally supposed to be haunted by a lady who took the form of a white dog.

Barnbougle Castle stands on the shores of the Firith of Forth to the west of Edinburgh. It is located within the parklands of Dalmeny House, to which estate it belongs. Here the Hound of Barnbougle is reputed to howl all night long each time a laird of the castle dies. The original hound was supposed to have howled in grief when his master, Sir Roger de Mowbray, left to fight in the crusades in the early thirteenth century. (Some folk say that its owner was Sir John Moubray.) Listening to its moans, he decided that he would take it on the trip with him. Sir Roger was later killed in battle, and on the night he fell the hound was heard baying on the promontory near Barnbougle, known since that time as Hound Point. Some folk claim that the dog managed to return home to Barnbougle by itself.

To the south of Edinburgh is Roslin, or Rosslynn, Castle, standing high on a rocky headland surrounded by the River North Esk. As at Barnbougle, the barking and baying of a dog is sometimes heard within the building. According to tradition the dog belonged to an English soldier who came to fight in the Scots wars of independence in 1302. When a Scots soldier killed its master, the dog began growling ferociously and barking. At length he was forced to kill the dog too. From that time the howling has been heard in Roslin Castle where it is known as the Mauthe Dog'.

A ghost horse with its rider is sometimes seen in the byways near to Littledean Tower near Melrose. The tower dates from the sixteenth century and possibly occupies the birthplace of John Duns Scotus, the celebrated thirteenth-century philosopher, beatified in 1993 by Pope John Paul II. The ghost on horseback is said to be a former laird of Littledean who killed a stable lad.

In the district round Edinburgh there are a number of other haunted castles. Borthwick Castle is a staunch towerhouse rising 80 feet in height with 14-feet-thick walls. Located a few miles from Gorebridge, it is now a hotel. The Red Room is haunted by a young girl, known as Ann Grant. She is supposed to have been a local peasant's daughter who became pregnant by a Lord Borthwick. 'To prevent the indignity of having an illegitimate heir, the laird is supposed to have murdered her. She has been seen a number of times in this room, but one of the castle's lessees, Helen Bailey, had the room exorcized after herself witnessing the figure. The ghost is thought to dislike men, understandably, for even when she is not visible, doors have been known inexplicably to slam shut on men's toes and fingers.

Pencait Castle stands six miles north-east of Borthwick, at the twin villages of Pencaitland. Known variously as Fountainhall and Woodhead, the castle is an attractive sixteenth-century tower house, originally owned by the Pringle family. Three ghosts have been noted here, and one of them is said to be of Charles I, though he has not been seen. People believe the Stuart king's spirit to be present, partly because one of his beds and his deathmask were kept here for many years. These were given to Sir Andrew Lauder in the 1920s and installed in what became known as King Charles' Room.

The second Pencait ghost is that of a beggar man, Alexander Hamilton, who was later hanged in Edinburgh for his part in murder and sorcery. A few days before he had sought sanctuary at the castle, only to be turned away. In a rage he cursed the castle and its occupant.

The third ghost is known as 'Gentleman John' because of his dapper appearance. The spirit was originally embodied by one John Cockburn, but legend fails to recall exactly whether he was murdered or committed suicide.

Within the western confines of Edinburgh stands the attractive Lauriston Castle, now one of the city's museums. Part of the building is a late sixteenth-century tower house to which a mansion was added in 1824, complete with secret doorways and hiding holes. According to many people the sound of a butler's shuffling feet dm be heard. There was formerly an aged manservant employed in the castle who used to waddle around the castle in his slippers. As far as I am aware, no one has actually seen the ghost.

Across the Firth of Forth from Edinburgh is the kingdom of Fife, home of many hauntings. Kellie Castle, now protected by the National Trust for Scotland, is just one location where ghosts have been seen. Standing three miles north west of Pittenweem, Kellie was first erected in 1360, but most of what we see today dates from the late sixteenth century. The Trust bought the castle in 1970 from the Lorimer owners, one of whose ancestors, Professor James Lorimer, who died in 1890, is said to haunt the building. His ghost is usually seen seated on a chair in one of the passageways.

A second ghost, which haunts the spiral staircase in the castle, originates from a much earlier time: Anne Erskine, whose family owned Kellie from 1613 until 1829 when the last Earl of Kellie died. She is said to have dashed up the spiral stairway and leaped to her death from an upper window. Her spirit is rarely seen, but the sound of her feet clattering on the treads has been heard quite regularly. At one time the castle was exorcized, but without great success.

Several castles in Scotland's south-western counties are apparently haunted. In Wigtownshire we have Baldoon and Galdenoch Castles. The former stands in ruins a mile south of the county town and is said to be haunted by a woman called Janet Dalrymple. Though betrothed to a Sir David Dunbar of Baldoon, she had a mind to marry another man. Her parents insisted that she marry Dunbar, for her preferred mate was the third son of a penniless lord. The ceremony went ahead, but on the wedding night when Sir David and the reluctant bride were alone in the castle Janet was mortally wounded and died soon after. No one knows whether she committed suicide, was murdered, or whatever, but her spirit has been said to haunt the castle from that time onward. Usually materializing in a wedding dress stained with blood, the apparition is most often seen on the anniversary of the wedding day. The story of Janet Dalrymple was used by Sir Walter Scott in his novel *The Bride of Lammermoor*.

Galdenoch Castle is located on the Rhins of Galloway, seven miles from Stranraer. It, too, is in ruins, having been built in the sixteenth century for the Agnews. The ghost said to haunt this castle was one of the few ghosts that seems to have taken pleasure in harming people. The old story, as recounted in the *Hereditary Sheriffs of Galloway* by

Sir Andrew Agnew in 1864, goes as follows:

The tenant's mother sat one morning at her spinning-wheel; an invisible power bore her along and plunged her in the Mill-Isle burn, a voice mumbling the while, 'I'll dip thee, I'll draw thee,' till the old dame became unconscious. Great was the surprise of the family at dinner-time when grandmamma was missed. Every corner of the buildings was searched; the good man and his wife became alarmed, while the lads and lassies ran madly about interrogating one another with, 'Where's granny?' At last a well-known voice was heard, 'I've washed granny in the burn and laid her on the dyke to dry!' Away the whole party ran; and sure enough the poor old woman lay naked on the dyke, half dead with cold and fright.

Several ministers tried to lay the spirit by psalm-singing; but if they sang, the spirit out-sang them. A minister who was considered an expert on spirit-laying was beaten like the rest, and, annoyed at his failure, declared that he would never come back. When the yard-gate had closed behind him, the voice begged him to return, promising to tell him something he had not heard before. Beguiled by curiosity, the minister did return, but only to hear the cry, 'Ha! Ha! I have gotten the minister to tell a lee!'

The farmer's family were now worse off than ever. The spinner's threads were broken short off; peat clots fell into the porridge; unsavoury materials were thrown into the kail-pot, when, after many years of trouble, a young man named Marshall, gifted with confidence and a stentorian voice, was ordained to the parish of Kirkcolm. He volunteered to try a bout with the Galdenoch ghost, and a large company assembled to assist. The minister hung up his hat, gave out a psalm, and led off the tune. The ghost sang, too; the company endeavoured to drown his voice, but failed; the fiend sang long and loud, and all had ceased but the minister, whose voice rose to a louder and louder pitch as he kept up the strains alone until the 'witching hour'. He called upon the wearied congregation to join once more. A burst of psalmody was the response; and 'Bangor', loud if not melodious, resounded through the castle-walls. Again all ceased exhausted, but Marshall undauntedly held on. Faint gleams of light streaked the eastern horizon, when the unearthly voice, husky and weak, whined 'Roar awa', Marshall, I can roar nae mair!', Marshall still continued, determined to make assurance doubly sure; but the ghost kept his word and was never heard again.

Carleton Castle stands on the hillside above the village of Lendalfoot in Ayrshire, twenty-eight miles south along the coast from the county town. A simple square keep of which one corner is missing, the ruins are said to be haunted by the spirit of Sir John Cathcart, described as 'Ayrshire's Bluebeard'. Infamous for his liking of women, he had a number of girlfriends, each one of whom he married. But after a short time he grew tired of them and pushed them over the Games Loup, one of the nearby sea-cliffs. Seven women were disposed of in this way. He had his comeuppance with his last bride, May Kennedy of Culzean. Suspecting what he was about to do, she pushed him over the precipice instead. His ghost is said to be heard screaming at Carleton Castle, as well as at Culzean.

Inland, following the River Girvan, we come at length to Cloncaird Castle, nestling in the hills between Straiton and Kirkmichael. The castle is basically a Gothic restoration of an old tower house that remains at the nucleus. There are two unusual spirits here. One is a figure that appears fairly regularly on the stairs, and the present owner of the castle, R. H. MacGregor, has become so used to the ghost that he is no longer frightened by its presence.

Culzean Castle, Ayrshire, is one of a number of places where a ghostly piper has been heard both in the castle and around the grounds.

The second unnatural phenomenon at Cloncaird is quite unique. In the games room, when billiards or snooker is being played, balls can be suddenly stopped or deflected for no apparent reason. It is as if some invisible hand is reaching over the table and knocking the balls as they are being played. This has happened many times, and is regarded as a recreational hazard.

In the north-east corner of the county stands the ruins of Loudoun Castle, described in the past as the 'Windsor of the North' from its appearance. The castle was haunted by a Grey Lady that once made regular appearances. Since the castle was burned down in 1941, the figure seems to have been rarely sighted. The Grey Lady was at one time such a common sight in the factor's office that he used to just ignore her.

Across the valley from Loudoun stands Cessnock Castle. Still inhabited today, it was at one time also owned by the Earls of Loudoun. The oldest part is the foursquare tower which dates from the beginning of the fifteenth century, or even earlier. Some of the walls are eighteen feet thick. Many famous folk from Scotland's history have visited Cessnock, including Robert Burns, Mary Queen of Scots and John Knox. Ghosts have been linked with the latter two.

Queen Mary arrived at Cessnock in her flight from Scotland after the Battle of Langside at Glasgow in 1568. She was accompanied by her ladies-in-waiting, one of whom died here. Her spirit is said to have remained in the castle, wandering through the rooms. The other ghost at Cessnock is said to be that of John Knox, whose spirit has appeared a number of times in the ancient tower, usually quoting the scriptures.

The ruins of Duchal Castle are fragmentary, but can still be found in Strathgryffe in

Renfrewshire. Anciently a Lyle seat, the castle was superseded by the present Duchal House of 1768. The ruin is the setting for a very old ghost story, recorded in the *Chronicle of Lanercost*. In the thirteenth century the spirit of an excommunicated monk was regularly seen here. He would rest on the outbuildings of the castle and hurl abuse at the residents. Several times the Lyles shot arrows at the cantankerous spectre to try and get rid of it, but apparently the arrows melted on contact with the form. One night the laird's son spotted the monk and decided to try and sort out the problem once and for all. He spent much of the night wrestling with the monk in the castle's great hall. Next morning the family found the son's dead body among the disturbed furniture and contents of the hall. Yet the Duchal ghost was never witnessed again.

A number of Scottish castles are haunted by ghostly musicians. Tales told about these spirits often have a common motif. In order to explore a secret tunnel fully, a musician is sent down to play the pipes or drums along the entire route so that those on the ground above can plot the direction of the underground passage. In most cases the minstrel gets lost, or is never seen again, but the sound of his music is still heard from time to time.

Culzean Castle in Ayrshire is one of the places where a piper ghost can be seen. He has been witnessed both in the castle and also on a woodland drive through the grounds known as Piper's Brae. Beneath the castle is a cave that is connected to the lower cellars of the building, and the piper is said to be heard in it. He is thought to be one of the early Kennedys who owned this castle since the origin of recorded history, though in 1945 it was passed to the National Trust for Scotland by the Marquis of Ailsa. Some say the piper is heard only before' one of the Kennedy family is about to get married.

Culzean has two more reported ghosts. One progresses through the house and is most often seen on the grand oval staircase. At times the crackling of fire and muffled screaming can be heard. The apparition of an attractive young woman, often dressed in an exquisite ballgown, has also been spotted in the castle.

In Lanarkshire stands Mains Castle, found on the outskirts of the New Town of East Kilbride. For many years in ruins, the castle has been restored as a family home by Michael Rowan. A folk tale records a former occupant of the castle having been strangled by her husband. The woman was a sister of King William the Lion and lived here with her husband, but she also had a secret lover. One day her husband arrived home unexpectedly so she was forced to conceal her lover within the tower. Later that night she lowered knotted sheets over the battlements to help her lover escape, but she was caught in the act and her husband slew her in fury. Locals claim that on some evenings visions of both the lady and the sheets manifest themselves.

Gight Castle in Aberdeenshire is home to another piper ghost. The ruins of the fifteenth-century castle stand above a deep glen of the Ythan Water, five miles from Fyvie. The usual tale of a secret passageway is related here, the piper having entered the tunnel to play his pipes never to be seen again. Naturally, the sound of his instrument is still heard on occasion.

A similar tale is common around Culross in Fife. Here a blind piper agreed to explore a secret tunnel said to extend from the abbey into a deep chamber where piles of gold and silver were reputed to lie untouched. He and his dog set off from a vault at the head of the Newgate. People followed the musician, blowing his pipes all the time, above ground. As they reached the West Kirk three-quarter of a mile away from their starting point, the music suddenly stopped. The piper was never seen again, though eerie tunes are said to echo below the village at times. The dog did manage to escape a mysterious fate, though according. to tradition it re-emerged in a terrible state of shock, with all its hair missing, and died soon after.

Cortachy Castle is the seat of the Earl of Airlie; it stands above the River South Esk, four miles north of Kirriemuir. The building has long been haunted by the spirit of a drummer that makes itself known when one of the family is about to die. In 1845 it was heard prior to the death of the Countess. Lord Airlie remarried in 1848 and at the wedding reception in the castle the sound of the drum was heard by one of the guests. When she told the newly married couple they both turned pale, for it meant that one of them was about to die. It turned out to be the new Countess, who expired shortly after in Brighton.

The drums were heard beating again in 1853, when the Earl himself, the ninth, died. His heir, David Ogilvy, tenth Earl of Airlie, died in 1881, and though he died in America, the sound of drums was heard at Cortachy a week beforehand.

The story behind the drummer goes back to the sixteenth or seventeenth century. He is said to have been the Ogilvy clan drummer, a young lad employed to beat the rhythm as they marched into battle. He was often in the presence of the laird, and through this connection he became acquainted with his wife. The drummer and the countess had an affair, but when the earl found out he had the youth thrown from the castle's battlements, along with his drum. The drummer survived his fall for long enough to curse the family, vowing to haunt the castle as long as the Ogilvys remained in possession.

In the Perthshire valley of Glen Lyon stands Meggernie Castle an attractive tower house of 1582. It was owned between 1689 and 1776 by the Menzies family, one of whom cut his wife's body in half after having accused her of seeing another man. He disposed of the body and then travelled to Europe. On his return he announced that his wife had died abroad—the perfect alibi. However, it was all for nought as he died within a short time. The ghost of the murdered wife has been seen several times in the castle on some occasions the head and torso, on others the waist and legs. At least once this figure has kissed someone lying in the bed of what has become known as the Haunted Room. After alterations to the castle in the late 1800s, workmen found the skeleton of an upper torso hidden beneath the floor in one of the rooms. These bones were buried in the nearby kirkyard, but the hauntings continued unabated.

Ethie Castle is situated in Angus, five miles north-east of Arbroath. The building dates from the fifteenth century, though earlier work was probably incorporated into the large and rambling building. Here the spirit of Cardinal David Beaton has been noted, usually within the so-called 'secret passage'. Beaton (born 1494) was the abbot of Arbroath Abbey and it was he who commissioned the building of the present castle, though some folk reckon it is older than his time. At any rate, he lived here for a number of years prior to his violent murder at St Andrews in 1546, since when his spirit has roamed through the building. Those who have seen him give a description of a small, fat and ruddy-complexioned figure, dressed in a red gown. That the cardinal suffered gout is evidenced by the ghost's clumping walk.

Ethie also houses the ghost of a young child, often heard playing with a toy. Sounds of crying, pattering feet and toys moving along the floor have all been marked. Investigations were made in the room where the child was most commonly heard and a small skeleton was discovered. With it were the fragments of a toy cart. Who the child was, or when he was killed, if that was his fate, is unknown.

Further up the coast from Ethie, at Inverbervie in Kincardineshire, stands Hallgreen

Castle, which is haunted by a spectre known as 'the Watcher'. The castle stands on a low headland at the southern end of Bervie Bay and was for a number of years uninhabited and falling into ruin. It was bought by Ian MacMillan, Baron of Brigfoord, who initiated a do-it-yourself restoration process in 1983, bringing the tower of 1374 back into a habitable condition. The Watcher is a male ghost who is usually seen wearing a long cloak, most often in a vaulted passageway. It gets its name from its staring look. Other ghosts have been seen in the castle since it was restored, including a woman who committed suicide after her child died in infancy, to two medieval servant girls who frequent a vaulted lower room. When they appear the room, usually turns a deathly cold.

The royal family's Highland home is at Balmoral Castle in Deeside, bought by Queen Victoria and Prince Albert and used for holidays ever since. The castle's paranormal credentials are disputed, but some claim that the spirit of Victoria's manservant, John Brown, has been seen in the building. After the death of Albert, John Brown became a close acquaintance of the queen, some even say a lover. Most accounts say that his ghost is usually seen in either the entrance hall or one of the corridors of the grand castle.

Just over two miles from Balmoral stands Abergeldie Castle, further down the River Dee from the royal seat. Dating in part from the sixteenth century, the castle has been lived in sporadically by various members of the royal family, but has remained in Gordon ownership. The ghost of a French maid is said to haunt the old tower and the sound of bells ringing and other noises have been heard emanating from the dungeon. The French maid, or 'Kitty Rankie' as she was known, was employed in the castle, but gained a reputation for dabbling in black magic. Once apprehended, she was tried, found guilty and then tied to a stake on the nearby hill of Creag nam Ban, where she was burnt in a bonfire. Her spirit has been seen in the castle on and off ever since, most often in the tall clocktower.

Aberdeenshire is famed for its Castles of Mar, most of which seem to be haunted. Castle Fraser dates from 1575 and was passed into the care of the National Trust for Scotland in 1976. The oldest part of the castle has a staircase with wooden treads. These were put down to cover a bloodstain that could not be removed from one of the underlying stone steps. According to tradition, some time at the end of the nineteenth century, a princess was murdered in the castle and her body dragged down the staircase before being buried in the grounds. As the corpse was taken down the stairs blood smeared on one of the steps and despite many scrubbings could not be removed.

Braemar Castle stands just outside the Highland village of the same name. Still owned by the Farquharsons of Invercauld, the castle is kept in excellent repair and is regularly open to the public. Built around 1628, the castle is haunted by a blonde woman, reputedly only appearing when the building is occupied by a honeymoon couple. She is said to be the spirit of a newly wed who stayed there with her young husband some time in the nineteenth century. The groom left early the morning after their wedding night to take part in a hunt, and when the bride woke she thought that he had left her. In her misery she threw herself to her death from the battlements. From that day on her spirit is said to appear at intervals. One of her most recent appearances was in 1987 when a young couple were spending part of their honeymoon in the castle as guests of Captain Farquharson.

A second ghost is also said to haunt Braemar. In 1689 the castle was torched by the 'Black Colonel', John Farquharson of Inverey, when the castle had been commandeered

Castle Fraser, Aberdeenshire, where the death of a princess resulted in bloodstains on a stair that could not be removed.

by the Master of Forbes and 150 soldiers on behalf of the government. It is said that his ghost sometimes returns, and though rarely seen, he is known to leave behind a burning candle to remind folk of his visit.

Another grand Castle of Mar is Craigievar, located on the side of a hill six miles to the south-west of Alford, also in Aberdeenshire. A very fine and unspoilt example of a tower-house, the castle of 1626 has also been acquired by the National Trust for Scotland. Within the tower is the Blue Room, haunted by the manifestation of a Gordon. He is said to have been pushed from a window by the third laird, 'Red' Sir John Forbes. His footsteps have been heard on the stairway.

A second apparition has materialized at Craigievar, when a crowd of strangers seem to appear in the Great Hall. According to some folk they appear when the Forbes family are in some kind of trouble, as if to offer help. Cecilia, Lady Sempill, widow of the nineteenth Lord Sempill, has witnessed these strangers. She noted that they were dressed in clothes of a dated fashion.

Delgatie Castle stands on the Aberdeenshire plain, just over two miles from the market town of Turriff. An ancient tower-house, it was considered unsafe and threatened with demolition before being restored by Captain John Hay of Hayfield and Delgatie. The tower rooms have interesting painted ceilings of 1593, 1597 and a

Right: Craigievar Castle, Aberdeenshire, where the haunted footsteps of someone are heard in the Blue Room.

Below: Delgatie Castle, Aberdeenshire, where the ghost of a romantic redhead is said to appear before bachelor visitors.

modern facsimile of 1955. The castle is haunted by the ghost of a vivacious redhead who is said to visit any bachelor who spends the night in the bedroom named after her, 'Romaise'. In history, Romaise is said to have successfully defended the castle during an attack.

Also in Buchan is Fedderate Castle, two miles north of New Deer. A stark ruin, the castle at one time had six storeys and was reached by a causeway over a wide bog. A seat of the Irvine family, the castle was taken by the Jacobites following the Battle of Killiecrankie. The fortress is said to be haunted, but there are few accounts of what the ghost looks like, or who the spirit was in its earthly life.

In the Aberdeenshire uplands, on the edge of the Grampian mountains, stands Corgarff Castle, maintained by Historic Scotland. Like Braemar, Corgarff was garrisoned by the government troops during the Jacobite uprisings and beyond. Earlier, in 1571, the castle was occupied by Margaret Forbes and her family, along with their servants and retainers. The castle was attacked by Adam Gordon of Auchindoun and his men whilst Lady Forbes' husband was away from home, and twenty-seven civilians were killed in all. Spirits whose identities are uncertain haunt the building, but it is reckoned that they originated from this massacre. Their screams have been heard echoing through the tower.

A National Trust for Scotland property, in the county of Moray, is Brodie Castle, four miles west of Forres. The castle is not generally thought to be haunted, but there is one supernatural incident associated with the place that should be mentioned. The twenty-third Brodie of that Ilk, Hugh, died on 20 September 1889 whilst in Switzerland. He had been staying at a spa seeking a cure for a serious illness. During his two-month absence the castle had been let out, but his servants had been warned that no one was to enter his private study, located on the ground floor. In any case it was left locked. One night the butler announced to the rest of the servants that he had heard someone moving about in the study. No one owned up to having been in the room, and as the door was still locked it was a genuine conundrum. The servants listened from behind the door of the study and heard the sound of moaning and rustling papers. In a perplexed state the household went to bed. Next morning word arrived that the Brodie had died the previous evening.

Only seven miles west of Brodie, but in the county of Nairn, stands the ruins of Rait Castle, haunted by a female figure known as the 'Wraith of Rait'. The castle is located due south of the county town and dates from the early fifteenth century. It was a seat of the Cumming, or Comyn family, who were for many years at feud with the Mackintoshes. On one occasion the Cumming chief invited the Mackintosh clan to a banquet at Rait, offering to forgive all past differences. In fact he planned to kill all the Mackintosh guests during the feast when a special signal was given. At the given sign, the Cummings rose and were on the point of attacking their guests when the Mackintoshes slipped out their dirks and killed the Cummings. Somehow they had been forewarned of the plans. The Cumming chief survived, and put the blame on his daughter, who was said to be in love with a Mackintosh. Indeed, some say the feast was convened to celebrate the pair's marriage. In the ensuing struggle the girl fell from the battlements to her death. Her spirit, dressed in bloodstained garments, is said still to roam around the castle.

Another ten or eleven miles to the west brings us to Castle Stuart, standing on a level plain in the parish of Petty, six miles from Inverness. A splendid baronial tower house, the castle contains a haunted room high up in one of the turrets. Little is known about

Above: Corgarff Castle, Aberdeenshire, has a number of spirits who are said to have originated at a massacre there in 1571.
Below: Brodie Castle, Moray, where strange sounds heralded the death of the laird who was abroad in Switzerland.

the ghost, but the room is available for letting and does attract intrepid residents!

Six miles north-east of Invergordon, in the county of Ross and Cromarty, stands Balnagown Castle. A fourteenth-century castle lies at the core of this massive Gothic pile. Balnagown was the seat of the chief of the Ross clan, but that family sold it in 1978 after over six centuries of ownership. Two ghosts haunt the building, one a sixteenth-century rogue, the other a Scots princess.

Andrew Munro, otherwise known as 'Black Andrew', was a landed gentleman in these parts. He carried the concept of droit de seigneur a little far, even for the middle of the sixteenth century, becoming notorious for rape and murder. He put the locality under such pressure that eventually the Ross chief captured and hanged him. Tradition has it that the corpse hung outside a high bedroom window in the castle's Red Corridor. His spirit has been seen walking this passageway. Some say he usually appears whenever a new lady visitor arrives at the castle. More often than not, only the sound of his footsteps can be heard.

The second ghost at Balnagown is said to be that of a Scots princess, supposedly murdered in the castle. A recent witness described the ghost as dressed in grey, with gold hair and green eyes.

Skibo Castle is located a few miles north of Balnagown, across the Dornoch Firth and in the neighbouring county of Sutherland. Famous as the home of the multi-millionaire philanthropist, Andrew Carnegie, the castle had a reputation before his time for being haunted. It is said that screams could be heard throughout the building, and the ghost of a woman running through the corridors has been seen. The phenomena apparently derive from a woman who once visited the castle when the laird was away from home, and only one of the male servants was in residence. The woman was never to return home, nor was her body ever found. The servant was suspected of murdering her, but no proof could be found, and after a time he moved elsewhere. One day workmen were repairing part of the castle and discovered bones hidden behind panelling. These were immediately thought to belong to the missing woman. After being decently interred in the local kirkyard the hauntings stopped.

Also in Sutherland is the ruined castle of Ardvreck, perched on a romantic promontory that butts into Loch Assynt. Haunting this building is the ghost of a Grey Man, remarkable for talking to those witnesses who have the nerve to answer back. The spirit speaks in Gaelic, and is said to be well informed of local goings-on.

On the Orkney island of Westray stands Noltland Castle, a fine Z-plan tower dating from 1560, but never completed. It is maintained by Historic Scotland and the ruins are open to the public. The castle was for many years a seat of the Balfour family, and it is said that a spectral light appears over the building each time a new child is born into that family or when one of them gets married. More ominous, however, is a howling dog, known as the 'Boky Hound', which is heard before one of them is about to die.

There used to be a friendly ghost at Noltland Castle when it was still occupied, but it has not been seen since the building fell into ruins. Known to the family as 'the Broonie', this ghost was regularly seen strolling through the castle and its gardens and studying things in great detail, as if to check that all was in order. At times he is said to have lent a hand to folk in trouble. The Balfours were quite enamoured of their spirit, and reckoned that he was looking after them.

On the island of Skye stand the ruins of Duntulm Castle, which dates from the fifteenth-century. At one time a seat of the MacLeods, Duntulm stands on a cliff top

Dunstaffnage Castle, Argyll, is claimed to be haunted by no fewer than thirteen ghosts.

near the northernmost tip of Skye. Duntulm became a possession of the MacDonalds and the ghost of one of them reputedly haunts it. According to old stories, when one of the MacDonald chiefs died Donald Gorm Mór, his son and heir, was disliked so much that most clansmen preferred the next in line, a cousin named Hugh or Uisdean, to succeed. A scheme was hatched whereby he would take the castle and kill the new chief. When the appointed hour arrived Hugh was captured himself and starved to death in one of the castle's turrets. His ghost frequented the building thereafter; indeed it is said that the hauntings became so intense that the MacDonalds abandoned the castle at the beginning of the eighteenth century.

Other ghosts are associated with Duntulm. The spirit of Donald Gorm Mór MacDonald himself is said to wander among the ruins, drinking whisky and ale and brawling with friends. His wife's spirit has also been seen, as has the ghost of a nursemaid who was murdered in revenge for an accident in which one of the MacDonald children she was supposed to be looking after accidentally fell from the castle cliff to its death on the rocks of Rubha Meanish.

Back on the mainland, to the north of Oban, stands Lochnell Castle, seat of the Earl of Dundonald. There is a 'Brownie' haunting the building, and the sound of supernatural music has been heard by a number of people.

Nearer to Oban, on the opposite side of Ardmucknish Bay, stands Dunstaffnage Castle, protected by Historic Scotland. A particularly fine example of a castle of enclosure or courtyard castle, the oldest parts date from the thirteenth century. According to tradition, the castle is home to no fewer than thirteen ghosts, the most notorious being Glaistaig, or Ell-Maid, who foretells good and bad times. She has been known to throw people sleeping from their beds. The sound of her footsteps is often heard, among those hearing them being Michael Campbell, twenty-second Captain of Dunstaffnage.

Farther down the Argyll coast, on the Kintyre peninsula, stands Saddell Castle. Restored in recent years and available for let through the Landmark Trust, the castle is home to a ghostly monk who is said to have come from nearby Saddell Abbey, along with many stones stolen from the ruins when the castle was built around 1508. The abbey lands were granted by James IV to David Hamilton, Bishop of the Isles.

Saddell has a second ghost, that of a White Lady. She has been seen looking over the crenellated battlements, but her identity has never been discovered. When she appears she is often accompanied by strange sounds, but sceptics claim these to be the wind whistling through the pipes of an old organ kept in the castle's attic.

6

OTHER GHOSTS

There are many other tales of ghosts from all over Scotland that do not fall into any neat grouping. This final chapter will detail many of these obscurities, but there are thousands of other weird happenings occurring every year that could also be listed. Space limits us to a selection.

The Grampian mountains are home to two famous ghosts, one the Grey Man of Beinn MacDuibh, the other a ghost that became celebrated after it was cited as evidence in a court of law. Much has been written on both cases, the former having been dealt with in great depth in *The Big Grey Man of Ben MacDhui*, by Affleck Gray, the latter in many magazine articles and chapters of books over the years. Even Sir Walter Scott wrote about the case in his *Letters on Demonology and Witchcraft*.

After the Jacobite rising of 1745 many English soldiers were sent to the Highlands to various garrisons to police the countryside. A regiment under Colonel Guise was sent to Deeside in 1749, where a group of eight men served under Sergeant Arthur Davies or Davis, as his name is sometimes spelled. Davies was an Englishman, but his good manners and sense of fair play won him respect and affection from many folk in the district. He had recently married and lived at that time at Dubrach farm near Inverey.

On the morning of 28 September Davies left early to spend a few hours hunting. He was to meet the rest of his patrol later at the head of Glen Clunie, where they usually had a sortie with a patrol stationed at the Spittal of Glenshee. However, Davies never made the meeting, for he was killed en route. His men met the other soldiers at the Cairnwell, but did not worry that the sergeant had not appeared, for he sometimes failed to keep his appointments. The patrol from Glenshee had met him on the way and were told that he intended hunting deer. That was the last time he was seen alive.

When Arthur Davies failed to return to his cottage his wife Jean raised the alarm. The patrol headed back up Glen Clunie in the general direction in which he had last been seen. They found no sign of him. The search parties persevered for four days before giving up. Some suggested that the sergeant had fallen out with his wife and secretly absconded back to England, but his wife was adamant that they were deeply in love and that he had talked of trying to win promotion.

In June 1750, nine months after the sergeant had disappeared, his ghost appeared in Glen Clunie to a shepherd named Alexander MacPherson. It stated: 'I am Sergeant Davies and I was murdered a year ago on the Hill of Christie.' The spirit asked MacPherson to give his bones a decent burial and to let Donald Farquharson know of his corpse's whereabouts. The apparition appeared a number of times to MacPherson, but he was frightened that the authorities would not believe him and perhaps blame him for the murder. At length, deeply troubled by the regular appearance of the ghost,

MacPherson sent word to Farquharson that he wished to speak to him. Farquharson was a son of the local laird of Invercauld, a great landowner in the district.

Farquharson did not believe MacPherson's story, but he realized that the man was deadly serious and that he would not get any peace until they had gone to the spot where the ghost said the body lay. They set off up the glen and in a peat bog found the skeleton of Davies, identifiable from some of its clothing. The two men buried the corpse in the peat.

A serious accusation was also made, for the ghost told MacPherson that the men responsible for its murder were Duncan Clerk, also known as Terig, and Alexander Bain MacDonald. Three years passed before the authorities were moved to try the pair, if only to put an end to the many rumours circulating in the glen. They were taken to the High Court of Justiciary in Edinburgh on 10 June, 1754. Lord Justice Clerk Alva and Lords Dunmore, Eɪchies, Kilkerran and Strichen presided. Interpreters were required to translate the Gaelic accounts for the benefit of the jury, which comprised Edinburgh businessmen.

Jean Davies was called first and identified the belongings as her husband's. Alexander MacPherson then told the court of his hauntings and of the demand that Donald Farquharson accompany him to bury the body. He also said that he had noticed Duncan Clerk had suddenly become much richer, and that he had taken on the lease of two farms. He offered MacPherson a job on them, which he accepted. The shepherd also saw Clerk's wife wearing a ring similar to one owned by Davies. Clerk had offered MacPherson £20 to help stock a farm if he would keep quiet about what he knew of Davies.

Other witnesses were called, among them Isobel MacHardie, who also claimed to have seen the ghost of a naked man enter MacPherson's house and go into his bedroom. John Grant said that Clerk had lodged with him the night before the murder and that Clerk had left that morning to shoot deer on a hill just a mile and a half from where Davies's body was found. Angus Cameron and a comrade, who were Jacobite fugitives and hiding among the hills, claimed to have seen Clerk and another meeting a man who resembled Davies and that two simultaneous shots were fired.

The lawyer for the defence had a difficult job of trying to clear Clerk and MacDonald, for the evidence was stacked against them. However, his trump card was to ask MacPherson what language the ghost had used when it spoke to him. MacPherson replied that 'It spoke as good Gaelic as myself which was seen as being most unusual for an Englishman! The doubt created by this anomaly was enough to force the jury to find the two not guilty and they were acquitted. No one was ever convicted for the sergeant's murder but his ghost seems to have finally rested in peace.

The Big Grey Man of Beinn MacDuibh, or Ben Macdhui as it is often spelled, has been noted for over a century. Probably the best-known, and earliest, account of this ghost was written up by Professor Norman Collie in 1891. He was a professor of organic chemistry at London University and a notable mountaineer, making many pioneering climbs throughout the country and being honoured by having Sgurr Thormaid (Norman's Peak) named after him in the Cuillin of Skye.

Collie was walking alone on the plateau of Beinn MacDuibh one spring morning in 1884. As his feet tramped on the snow he became aware of footsteps behind him. When he halted and turned round; the footsteps also stopped and there was not a thing to be seen. He walked on and again the sound of footsteps could be heard following him. He then realized that they only occurred every second or third step of his own. Turning once more, he was unable to find any source for the noise. Totally unnerved, he descended as fast as he could from the plateau into the lower reaches of the mountains in the Forest of Rothiemurchus.

One evening in June 1890 Dr. A. M. Kellas and his brother were on the slope of the mountain. The latter walked on ahead to the summit cairn. At one point the doctor looked up and saw a tall grey figure standing with his brother at the cairn; when he caught up with him he asked him who the strange-looking man had been. The brother replied that there had been no one there at all, only himself.

Another climber, Hugh Welsh, experienced the footsteps of the Big Grey Man, or An Fear Liath Mhór, as he is known in Gaelic. Whilst on the plateau—the highest in Britain, at over 4000 feet—in the summer months of 1904, he spent some time camping with his brother there. The Welsh brothers heard the footsteps of the Grey Man on their first overnight stay, yet could find no sign of the source when they clambered out of the tent to look. At a, different time, and during daylight, they experienced the footsteps again.

In the 1920s Tom Crowley, president of the Moray Mountaineering Club, was climbing on Beinn MacDuibh when he heard the footsteps behind him. Like most witnesses, he reckoned the steps were of someone much larger than himself, from the sound they made as they trampled the ground. He turned round to see if someone was following him and was surprised to see in the distance a tall figure walking towards him. He described it as grey, with long legs, sharp talons and pointed ears. Its unnatural appearance terrified him and he ran as fast as his own legs could carry him.

In 1941 a woman named Wendy Wood experienced the phantom footprints whilst walking through the Lairig Ghru, a major pass through the Cairngorm mountains to the west of Beinn MacDuibh. She heard the sound of them behind her, and also the deep and resonating voice of a large man. The steps were out of phase with her own, and the sound occurred at a different rate, which meant that they were not just an echo of her own boots on the rock. Seeing no one in view she fled from the pass as fast as she could go.

The mountaineer and poet Syd Scroggie experienced the Grey Man in 1942. He was standing at the Shelter Stone in Coire Etchachan, looking down over Loch Etchachan, when he saw a tall figure appear from the mist in the distance and disappear at the other side of the glen. Curious, he went to where the figure had been, but could see no footprints and no reply came when he shouted.

Another person to have seen the figure was Alexander Tewnion in October 1943— again in Coire Etchachan. As he walked along the path in the mist he heard the sound of footsteps behind him. He had a gun with him, so he brought it out. Turning, Tewnion saw a tall human shape behind him, but one which did not seem natural. He shot at it three times and ran down the glen. No body was ever found.

Many other accounts of a tall grey-coloured figure have been given by climbers who have been in the vicinity of Beinn MacDuibh. In 1914 George Duncan, high sheriff of Aberdeen, saw a tall figure as he drove along the road in Glen Derry. It seemed to be dressed in a long cloak and was waving its hands at him, but eventually disappeared. A journalist from *The Times* reckoned that he had been chased by a sinister being. A man from Banchory in Kincardineshire saw the Grey Man in 1950. Joan Grant heard the sound of steps, described as hooflike, in the Forest of Rothiemurchus in 1982.

An old tradition in the Grampian mountains has it that the Big Grey Man is the ghost of William Smith, or Uilleam Ruighe Naoimhe, a poet and author of the song Allt an Lochain Uaine'. Though he is said to have died whilst climbing in the hills this is not true, for he had active service in the Peninsular War and died at Portsmouth in the south of England.

Another haunted mountain is Schiehallion, or Sidh Chaillean—the fairy hill of the Caledonians. Located south of Loch Rannoch, the mountain, when viewed from the east, is almost a perfect cone. There are many tales linking it with fairies and the little people, and the remains of a supernatural well visited on May Day are located on its slopes. Schiehallion has also been the haunt of a phantom hound.

Other ghosts have been seen amongst the mountains. At the Corrieyairack pass in the Monadhliath mountains is a ghost that seems to help travellers who have lost their way. Accounts tell of people walking across the pass, formed by General Wade as a military road, and seeing the spirit. He often announces to people, 'The road to Fort Augustus lies just ahead on the left,' and other such statements. Mr and Mrs Liddell were walking in the pass in the late 1940s and were given the above directions by a kilted Highlander. They walked down to Garbha Bridge, where they met a local man who asked if they had met the 'Ghost of the Corrieyairack'. They replied that they had. The local asked if he had dogs with him. Mrs Liddell thought that he was accompanied by two deerhounds, but her husband was adamant that he did not. It seems that the phantom dogs are usually only witnessed by females.

Other deerhounds that appear as ghosts have been seen in the Kirkton Glen at Balquhidder. This was an old, drovers' route that ran from Glen Dochart in the north through the mountains to Loch Voil and thence to Callander. Accounts of ghosts go back to at least the mid 1800s when Donald Ferguson, farmer at Kirkton, experienced phantom hunters with dogs passing through a wood. More recent witnesses saw a figure holding a long rifle dressed in ancient Highland clothes and with two dogs at his side. The two men split up and walked round a rocky outcrop, but by the time they met up on the other side the figures had disappeared.

A phantom hound known in Gaelic as An Cu Glas Mheobail, the grey dog of Meoble, haunts the countryside round about Arisaig, on the west coast of Inverness-shire, near Mallaig. It is supposed to terrorize humans: the tale behind its hauntings is repeated in many folk cultures around the world. Perhaps the oldest account of it can be found in the writing of Catwg Ddoeth, or Cadog the Wise, a fifth-century Welsh saint. The most common version locates the incident in Beddgelert, Wales, where the dog's grave is a popular tourist attraction. The stones, however, were set up only two centuries ago by an innkeeper that wished to improve his trade.

According to one version of the tale passed down through the years at Arisaig, a crofter's wife left her child in a cot at the door of their cottage as she went to draw water from the well. Their collie dog lay by the side of the cot, but when the woman returned she was horrified to find the child dead, its body chewed and ripped to pieces. The collie was covered in blood, some of which was dripping from its mouth.

The wife screamed to her husband, who, in a rage, killed the dog instantly by beating it to death with his stick. After having made sure it was dead, he found the corpse of a wolf at the end of the croft house and realized that the wolf had attacked the child but that the dog had, too late, forced it away from the baby and managed to kill it. Filled with remorse, the crofter had his dog buried decently.

Another version of the origin of the grey dog states that it was a deerhound owned by a Dougal MacDonald. When he went to fight in the Peninsular Wars his dog was left at home with his wife. After a time the dog ran off and made its own den on an islet in Loch Tain Mhic Dhughaill. There it brought up four pups, which were extremely wild due to their lack of human training. When the master returned home he was told of his dog's whereabouts. He set off to look for it, but on landing on the islet found the hound away from its lair. The four wild pups attacked him and ripped his body into little pieces. The mother later returned to the island where it saw its master's body. So distressed was she that she howled for hours on end. The noise attracted the locals, who, on investigating, also found the body of MacDonald. He was buried at Rifern on Loch Morar. The pups were killed by a local group of hunters.

The hound survived, and for many months lay on its master's grave, baying in grief. After a time the dog itself died. All was quiet for a time until the brother of Dougal MacDonald was ill in bed. Just before he died the hound made an appearance at his croft, howling loudly. It disappeared after a short time and the brother died.

The ghost of the dog is said to wander among the wooded glens of the parish of Arisaig. It tends to appear to those who are on their deathbeds, no matter where they are, so long as they are related to the MacDonalds. As well as appearing in Oban, Glasgow and elsewhere, in Scotland it has also materialized in front of descendants in Canada, where many Scots people emigrated.

At Clachtoll near to Lochinver on the western coast of Sutherland, yet another black dog is said to roam the moors. It is most often seen on the rocks of Creag an Ordain. The dog is said to have bright red eyes, likened to smouldering peat, a semi-human face, and horns on its forehead. The dog is said to laugh like a human, but should you hear it bark more than once death is reckoned to strike you soon after.

A ghostly white horse haunts Clumly Farm, which is located four miles to the north of Stromness in Orkney. According to the traditional tale, a young woman came to work on the farm some time in the late nineteenth century. The farmer had two sons, both of whom fell in love with her. The woman took what she could from both men, and played one off against the other to such an extent that they ended up hating each other.

One day in the barn, whilst threshing oats, one of the sons struck the other with a flail, cracking his skull open and killing him. He hid the body until later that day, when he stole a white horse from the byre. With the corpse tied over the horse the man rode to the cliffs at Yesnaby, where he disposed of the body. Returning to the farm he felt that he was being pursued by the ghost of the dead man. He pushed the horse into a gallop and rode home as fast as he could. At one point the horse's hooves struck a stone dyke that they were crossing, causing many stones to fall over. It is said that no one has since been able to repair that part of the dyke.

The phantom horse and rider have been seen many times at Clumly over the years, most often on wild and stormy nights. One day a woman at a farm near to Clumly answered her door to find the horse and man outside. However, they soon disappeared.

It is not merely human figures and animals that appear as ghosts. Phantom cars and other vehicles have also been seen on the byways of Scotland, and several have been blamed for road accidents. Typical of the ghostly cars that cause accidents is the one which makes its appearance on the A7 near Stow in Midlothian. Several drivers have followed what they thought was a real car only to run into a wall at the roadside. The phantom vehicle had just passed through it, following what had been an earlier route taken by the road.

On the island of Benbecula in the Outer Hebrides another vehicular manifestation has been seen a vintage car has been experienced by some drivers, and it too has caused a few accidents.

On the misty island of Skye a third automobile ghost has been recorded. It usually appears on the road from Sconser to Drynoch via Sligachan (the A850 and A863). Many folk have noted its lights driving towards them as they make their way in the opposite direction. After pausing in passing places, or driving round corners with extreme caution, the motorist is puzzled to discover that there is no vehicle there, and no side road down which the car could have turned. The same ghostly car was once noted in the daytime near to Drynoch. It was motoring across the moor when it suddenly vanished.

On the road to the isles, between Invergarray and Kyle of Lochalsh, the A87, a phantom car has been seen many times in Glenshiel—most often on the old section of road, before the present, wider road had been pushed through the narrow glen. Many motorists in the first half of the twentieth century spotted a car in the distance coming towards them. The vehicle would then disappear as it rounded a bend, but when the motorist who saw it drove round the bend from their side, he or she found that the road was clear. He or she would also note that there were no roads that the other vehicle could turn down, nor would it have had enough time to about-turn and head back whence it came. Among the many people who saw this phantom car was a university professor from Glasgow, who witnessed it twice in his life.

At Swinton, Berwickshire, in November 1977 a car was being driven along a minor road in the area when suddenly a large dark figure, dressed in a long cloak with a hood, stood in front of the vehicle. The driver slammed on the brakes, but he was quite sure that he had not stopped quickly enough and that he had hit the figure. On getting out of the car, he ran round the front to discover that there was no one there, nor any sign of damage to his car. This type of story is popular throughout the country, if not the world; a variant is that the driver sometimes finds only blood on the roadway when he gets out the car. In every case the spectre disappears just as quickly as it had appeared.

A phantom bus has been spotted a number of times in East Lothian. This vehicle travels from Prestonpans along the B1348 towards Cockenzie, but it never seems to have any passengers in it. Between Stow and Heriot on the A7 south of Edinburgh a ghost lorry also has been reported a number of times, driving up the valley of the Gala Water.

There are at least two known cases of ghost trains making their appearance in Scotland. The most famous is the one that travels across the Tay Bridge, or at least across the former Tay Bridge, which collapsed on 28 December 1879, killing seventy-five passengers and crew. Each year on the anniversary of the disaster, a phantom engine is said to pull its carriages across the line taken by the bridge, the taillight disappearing just where the train lunged into the estuary and the girders collapsed.

More remote is the ghost train that materializes at the former station of Dunphail, in the county of Moray. This railway was part of the Highland Line, but the route was closed many years ago and the track dismantled. The ghost train passes through what was the station, somehow running a few feet above ground level. The train was witnessed by John MacDonald in 1921, when the track still existed. He had been walking along the line shortly after midnight, at a time when he knew there were no trains. Many years later he discovered that his mother had seen the same phantom train on a different occasion, also floating above the rails. In more recent times, after the rails were lifted, folk have been blown off the track bed as if a train has shot past.

There are a number of churches and other religious buildings said to be haunted. Many of them are in ruins, but some remain in use. The old parish church of Dalarossie is romantically located in the valley of the River Findhorn, twenty miles from Inverness. Every time Christmas Day falls on the Sabbath ghosts are said to materialize here. They are involved in a game of football or shinty, depending on which account is read, played on the kirk's glebe. According to tradition, the Shaws of Strathnairn challenged the Mackintoshes of Strathdearn to a game on Christmas Day. However, when it was realized that Christmas fell on the Sunday the Strathdearn men did not turn up. The Shaws, not wishing their day to be spoiled, picked teams among themselves and had an enjoyable day. However, within the year, all of the participants had died mysteriously and were interred in the kirkyard.

Kilcormack is an ancient burial ground located on the banks of the River Dee, between Castle Douglas and Kirkcudbright. There are said to be ghosts here that rise from the dead in order to work the sluices and dams supplying the mill of Kilcormack. According to an ancient tradition, the fairies grind their corn on Hallowe'en, enough to last them all year. But as they cannot cross running water they use the resurrected corpses from the kirkyard to assist them when required. The mill at Kilcormack was tenanted by the Thomson family in the late eighteenth and early nineteenth centuries. James Thomson told an antiquarian in 1827 about his own experiences of the ghosts, as well as those related to him by his father and grandfather. Thomson's grandfather awoke in the middle of the night to hear the sound of his millwheel turning. Knowing what night it was, and what traditionally happened on such a date, he tried to ignore it and go back to sleep. His wife also heard the sounds, however, and forced him to get up and see what was happening. Reluctantly he did so, taking his collie dog with him. He saw the fairies and spirits, but when both he and his dog refused to partake of their meal they disappeared. On returning to bed a door slammed, jamming the collie's head and killing it.

Thomson's father was also disturbed in the middle of the night. He went down to the mill in order to close the sluice at the dam, but as he did so two ghostly hands grabbed him by the shoulders and pushed him back to his bed. From that day until his death, Thomson's father was reckoned to have shoulders so cold that nothing could get them to heat up.

James Thomson experienced the ghosts himself, though not as he slept. He was walking through some nearby fields when he saw a figure in old-fashioned clothes walking about the kirkyard. The manifestation passed through the gate and across a field of cattle to the mill dam. The cows did not seem to sense the figure's presence, but Thomson's dog was aware that something was there. It ran back to the millhouse, where it hid beneath a bed. When Thomson had a look in the kirkyard he realized that the spirit had appeared at a gravestone commemorating a miller who had died in 1578.

The kirkyard of Sanquhar in Dumfriesshire was formerly haunted by the ghost of Abraham Crichton, a merchant in the village and laird of Carco. He was declared bankrupt in 1741 and was later responsible for helping to demolish the ancient kirk of Kirkbride. His death by falling from a horse was seen by many as a judgement for his sins. Buried in the kirkyard of Sanquhar, his restless spirit would not remain in the grave and rq'ved about the parish. He was most often seen in the kirkyard or around the parish glebe. Eventually no one would pass the church at night for fear of being pursued.

The spirit became so popular that a small booklet was published on its exploits and was even discussed in Edinburgh literary circles.

It was eventually decided that a minister had to be found who could lay the ghost to rest. A Revd Hunter, incumbent at Penpont in the same county, agreed to perform the task. He spent a whole day in prayer and went to the kirkyard at midnight, armed with a sword in one hand, his Bible in the other. Next morning he refused to tell anyone what had happened during the night, but tales' of him marking out 'charmed circles' on the ground with his sword soon spread throughout the parish. The grave of Crichton was covered over by a large 'thruch-stane', chained to the ground. His spirit has never been seen since.

The old kirkyard of Kilneuair, or *cill an Iubhair* in Gaelic, stands by the side of Loch Awe in Argyll. Built into the wall of the kirk, which is now in ruins, is a stone lintel that some say is impressed with the handprint of a ghost, though others claim that the markings were made by the devil. Both accounts, however, are similar.

Kilneuair had a reputation for being haunted, but a tailor who lived nearby disbelieved all such tales. He bet his colleagues that he could spend the night in the church, and to pass the time he would make himself a pair of trousers. As he was busily working around midnight, a skeletal hand appeared from the floor of the church. A voice was heard, 'Do you see this great hoary hand, tailor?' He answered in the affirmative and said that he would continue to sew his trousers. A skull appeared next, and the voice asked again if he could see it. Similar questions were put to the tailor as other bones appeared, but he managed to remain reasonably calm. However, when the full skeleton appeared from the grave the tailor was seized by such fright that he grabbed his sewing and fled from the church. As the skeleton lunged at the tailor, a mark was left on the stone where it remains to this day.

The island of Tiree has two haunted kirkyards Kenovay and Sorobaigh. Kenovay is located near to the Bay of Balephetrish, the chapel ruins standing amid the rocky landscape. The burial ground is home to the manifestation of a seaman whose ghost was seen here at the moment he died. It has reappeared many times since. The sailor was drowned at sea, and his body was washed ashore and buried in the kirkyard.

Sorobaidh, or Soraby, kirkyard is haunted by Black John Campbell, a tax collector on behalf of the dukes of Argyll. He is said to have taken two plough horses in lieu of tax from a farm, whose owner was visiting the smithy at the time. The wife insisted frantically that the horses were worth much more than the tax owed, but her pleas fell on deaf ears. A stable boy overheard the argument and ran to the blacksmith's to tell the farmer. He, with a number of other men, pursued Black John into the kirkyard. Campbell stumbled and fell headlong across a tombstone. Pleading for his life, he promised that he would return the horses. The farmer and his associates meaning only to frighten the tax collector, accepted his offer. Though Black John did not die at that time, it is said that his ghost can be seen spreadeagled over gravestones in the kirkyard. This is located at the northern end of the village of Balemartine, at the end of Bagh Shorobaidh.

The chapel of St Matthew at Rosslyn, or Roslin, in Midlothian is famous for its 'Prentice Pillar'. Erected in 1450 this stone pillar is far superior in workmanship and design to all the other pillars in the building. It is said that William Sinclair, third Earl of Orkney, asked a mason to construct one in accordance with a sketch of a column in Rome. The master mason tried unsuccessfully, so went on a trip to Italy to inspect the original. Whilst he was gone his apprentice studied the sketch and began work himself.

He was keen and laboured with vigour, producing a pillar far better than any his master could have done. It boasted a riband of carved foliage winding round the ribs. When the master returned and saw how he had been outshone he is said to have killed the youth in a jealous rage.

Some say that the apprentice still haunts Rosslyn, indeed hundreds of folk claim to have seen him. Many say that he stands by the side of his work crying. There are three heads carved in the roof of the west chapel that are said to represent the mason, the apprentice and his distressed mother. The story is given further credence by the fact that the chapel could not be consecrated because a murder had taken place there. It required an Act of Reconciliation from the archbishop of St Andrew's before this could take place.

St Mary's Church in Haddington is said to be haunted by the spirit of John, first Duke of Lauderdale. He died in 1682 and was laid in the family burial aisle, though his spirit is said to wander around the church. For many years the coffin of the duke, and others belonging to his family, mysteriously moved around within the vault. Each time the mausoleum was unlocked to allow a further burial, the coffins would be found in a different position. For many years this caused quite a sensation in the district until it was realized that the vault lay below the flood level of the river. When the River Tyne was in spate the water table in the vault rose, causing the coffins to float around.

The ruins of St Andrews Cathedral in Fife are dominated by a rectangular tower, said to be the home of ghosts. Known as the Haunted Tower, it has two storeys and is built into the priory wall overlooking the coast. In 1868 the upper room of the tower was opened for the first time for many years; great was the surprise when it was discovered to contain many coffins and skeletons. One of these wore a pair of white leather gloves, just like the White Lady that has been witnessed in the cathedral yard.

The White Lady of St Andrews has been seen many times, most often in the late nineteenth century, though in 1975 she was seen by two people in the kirkyard, near to the tower. At first they thought it was a real person. However, the manifestation, wearing white gloves and a veil, walked towards them and promptly disappeared. Accounts of the White Lady and other spirits hereabouts were recorded in a book entitled *St Andrews Ghost Stories* by William T. Linskill (1856–1929), Dean of Guild in the town.

Another ghost haunts the grounds of St Andrews Cathedral, that of a monk. He was seen in the 1950s by a visitor to St Rule's Tower, which affords panoramic views of the town. As the visitor was climbing the winding stairs he tripped on the old stone treads and stumbled. As he righted himself he noticed a figure further up the staircase, dressed in a cassock. Asking the visitor if he was all right, the phantom monk offered to take his arm to help him mount the stairs. The visitor refused his help and had to squeeze past him to reach the top of the tower. When he got there he realized that he had not felt the monk as he crossed him on the narrow flight. After coming down, he asked the custodian if someone else had come out of the tower, only to be answered in the negative. The custodian and the visitor then realized that the ghostly monk of the cathedral must have made another visitation.

In 1979 a group of students witnessed three monks walking across the playing fields of St Andrews University. The monks were not walking on the grass, but were suspended about ten feet above the ground. It was a fine autumn night when the spirits were seen.

Melrose Abbey, Roxburghshire, is said to be haunted by the wizard Michael Scott.

Another phantom monk is said to haunt the road between Kilchrenan and Ardanaiseig, on the northern side of Loch Awe in Argyll. In the forest just over a mile from Kilchrenan is a large roadside boulder that was formerly used for sacrificial purposes. It is in fact a cup-marked rock, probably dating from the Bronze Age. A monk is said to have been captured and killed on this spot by Druids, and his headless body has been seen on occasion by passers-by.

The ruinous abbey of Melrose in the Borders is said to be the haunt of noted scholar Michael Scott, claimed by some to have been a wizard. After his death in 1292 he was interred here. He gained a reputation as a magician and necromancer, and his book of spells was supposedly buried with him. Some say his spirit haunts the eastern side of the abbey in the form of a serpent, or at least crawls along the ground in the same manner. Other accounts claim that this spirit is that of a monk who turned to crime and even vampirism.

Rathen is a rural parish near Fraserburgh in Aberdeenshire. The present church dates from 1870 and replaces an earlier building that stands in ruins with its kirkyard. An old tale states that this church was haunted by a ghostly choir. Each Sunday, whilst morning prayers were in progress, a choir could be heard singing in an upper loft, yet no one could be found there, let alone a group of singers. The singing was accompanied by an organ and other instruments. Several such experiences occurred in 1644, and a contemporary account refers to the phenomenon: 'About tyme of morneying prayer for diverse dayes together, hard in the church a queire of musicke, both of woces, organes and other instruments... People used to heare service, but they could sie nothing.'

Trumpan Church at Vaternish in Skye is also haunted by the sound of a singing congregation. The church is today in ruins, having been burned down in 1580 by the MacDonalds of Clan Ranald whilst some of the MacLeod clan were at worship. It is said that only one woman got out of the church alive. Though badly injured, she raised the alarm and the MacLeods who were still alive managed to kill their enemy before they could make their escape. Every year on the anniversary of the massacre, it is said that a spectral congregation continue their singing and service of praise in the church.

An archdeacon apparently visited the district soon after the Second World War and lived in a guest house near to the kirk ruin. One Sunday morning he awoke to hear the sound of voices singing in unison. From his knowledge of religious music he could tell that they were singing a Gregorian chant, a style out of favour for several centuries. At first he thought it was a radio he could hear, but his landlady assured him that no one in the district possessed one, and that in any case they would not play it on the Sabbath.

At Fortingall in Perthshire twelve ghostly nuns are reputed to walk through the small village. Where they come from or where they are heading, no one knows. The kirk does have an old monk's bell within it, however.

Perhaps the most sacred and religious spot in Scotland is the island of Iona, located off the westernmost tip of Mull. Here Columba arrived in Scotland from Ireland and began preaching to the residents of the western highlands and islands. There are a number of ghosts on the island, from monks to Viking longboats. The monks have been seen all over the island, but naturally appear most often near to the cathedral. Also in the cathedral the sound of tolling bells and phantom music has been heard. The appearance of ghost ships at Iona sailed by the Norsemen seems to happen less regularly. The ships have been witnessed by some folk sailing into the bay at Am Baile and re-enacting raids on the cathedral that may have occurred during the time Vikings attacked Scotland.

Partially linked to a church is the tale of a ghost that once haunted a wood near to Mosstodloch in Moray. The spirit was that of Alexander Gillan, hanged there in 1810. Gillan was an orphan employed as a farm labourer, and he was also something of a simpleton. He fell in love with a neighbouring farmer's daughter, but after a time they quarrelled and she would have nothing more to do with him. One day a few weeks later, Gillan was making his way to the church of Speymouth, half a mile from Mosstodloch. As he passed over the moor he met the girl's younger sister, Elspet, herding her father's cattle. In his rage, and blaming the girl for her sister's waning interest, he began to throw rocks at her. So furious was he that the stoning actually killed her. He continued on his way to the church.

Later that day as others walked back over the moor to their homes the body of the young girl was found. The outcry was immense, and suspicion quickly fell on Gillan, who had been agitated throughout the sermon. He was approached by the minister and, after questioning, confessed. He was taken to jail in Inverness where his trial was to take place. The circuit judge sentenced him to be hanged on the spot where he had committed the evil deed. The gallows were thus set up on the moor and he was suspended from the neck. The judge ordered that he be left suspended until the birds had eaten his flesh and the sun bleached his bones.

After a few weeks the corpse of Gillan mysteriously disappeared. The soldiers from Inverness arrived to search for it but there was no sign. From this time on, reports of Gillan's ghost were recorded. Many folk walking over the moor claimed to have experienced the manifestation pursuing them, and most people taking the shortcut began to give the site of the gallows a wide berth. The gallows and cage, used for the execution, remained *in situ* until 1911. In the same year locals petitioned the Duke of Richmond and Gordon, the local laird, to have them removed. He ordered that they be taken down and buried on the spot. As the men dug into the ground they found the skeleton of a young man, which turned out to be Gillan's. His corpse was reburied and the cage and gallows were placed over him before the whole trench was once again filled. From that day the spirit of Gillan has not been seen. The moor has since been planted with trees, but a path running through it is still known as Gillan's Way.

Ghosts turn up in many odd places. The building erected in 1931 as the main offices for Ayr County Council stands at the end of the fine Georgian Wellington Square in the county town. The site occupied by the buildings was formerly the county gaol, and the Sheriff Courthouse still stands alongside. The buildings are haunted by a headless figure that most folk agree was a former prisoner at the Bridewell. He is most often witnessed in the finance department and it is speculated that he is headless because he was executed there.

In Cathcart Street, also in Ayr, can be found a shop currently used as a kitchen showroom. The store was originally used as a branch of the British Linen Bank and a top-hatted gentleman, who might have been a bank manager, still haunts the premises. Soon after the building was converted in 1993 the owner and other members of staff became aware of some strange goings-on. They have heard voices and footsteps in the building when they knew that the place was empty, and have experienced objects being moved from one place to another. A cleaner, Marie Stewart, was the first to see the bank manager in the summer of 1994. She 'felt' that there was someone in the room with her and when she turned round she saw a tall man wearing a dark cloak and a top hat. At first she thought it was one of the staff playing a practical joke on her, but when she looked a second time the figure had totally vanished.

There are a few haunted theatres in Scotland. The Theatre Royal in Glasgow's Hope Street was erected in 1867. Today it is the home not only of Scottish Opera but also of a former cleaner's spirit who worked there. She has been named Nora by those who have witnessed her rare appearances.

At Glenrothes in Fife is the Rothes Hall Theatre, built on the site of an old burial ground. Workers there have reported ghostly occurrences over a number of years. Many of these incidents have been impossible to explain. The hall is used each week by a group of spiritualists, who claim that there are in fact three different ghosts in the building.

His Majesty's Theatre on Aberdeen's Rosemount Viaduct was erected in 1904 and is haunted by a former stagehand known as Jake. He was killed by a hoist some years ago, and his spirit lingers in the theatre to this day.

Also in Aberdeen is the tale of 'the Clencher', a spirit which haunts Union Street, the city's main shopping area. 'The Clencher' is claimed to be the ghost of a young girl who was murdered sometime in the nineteenth century. The murderers had actually been trying to kill her father, but the girl clung on to one of the miscreants with such force that she had to be cut off. The ghost of the girl, Victoria MacDonald, does not seem to be visible to anyone, but many folk have reported feeling her gripping their bodies tightly as they walk down the street. In many cases the mark of tiny hands is left on the victims' skin. The earliest-known report of this paranormal activity appeared in a newspaper of 1842. The account records that a Mary O'Hara was grabbed by something as she entered Union Street from Thistle Street. The marks of handprints were still visible on her arms four days later, yet Miss O'Hara saw no one. Reports of 'the Clencher's' activities are still being made to this day.

A transport café in Dundee is haunted by a man who is thought to have been a lorry driver employed in an old jute mill that used to occupy the same site. A number of unnatural experiences have taken place at the cafe, from items being shifted within the building overnight to half-eaten items of food being left on the tables after the place has been cleaned and locked up for the night. Whoever or whatever was responsible for the disruption did not set off the café's burglar alarm. Once the spirit left two pre-decimal pennies in payment for a chocolate bar which it had consumed. On another occasion in 1992 two workers at the café downed tools and left because of the ghost's activities.

A former cinema in Motherwell's Windmillhill Street is haunted by a weird spirit that has been nicknamed 'Oscar'. He actually predates the cinema, which was built in 1936, having come from the New Century Theatre which stood there before. According to one story, the ghost belonged to a man who had committed suicide by jumping from the theatre's balcony. The building is now used as a snooker club and the spirit seems finally to have found peace.

In nearby Wishaw is a factory said to be haunted by the ghost of Willie Primrose. A general handyman in the factory just before the Second World War, he was rather fond of the bottle. One Friday he found himself accidentally locked in to the boiler room when the factory closed down for the weekend. Returning to work on Monday morning, the workers found his dead body. From that time there were several reports of weird happenings in the building, from lifts working by themselves to machines switching on and off when no one was near. The ghost of the handyman was never seen, as far as I am aware, and it is said that he stopped haunting the works as soon as the person responsible for locking him up died himself.

The Glasgow Underground station at Shields Road on the south side of the river at Kingston is haunted by a Grey Lady. According to the tale, she was killed by a train in 1922 after having fallen on to the line. She was carrying a young child with her at the time, but the stationmaster is said to have rescued the little girl in a heroic manner. When workmen were repairing the track in the tunnel they heard the sound of footsteps in the distance, and on one occasion weird lights were seen between two groups of maintenance men.

There are a few tales linking ghosts to hospitals. Hawkhead Hospital in Paisley was established as a centre for infectious diseases and mental illnesses in 1935. A local story has it that the building was haunted by a Grey Lady, reputed to be a former ward sister who was murdered by one of the patients. This ghost is rarely, if ever seen, and may just be a myth told in the district to frighten the children.

At Glencorse Barracks on the south side of Edinburgh the ghostly figure of a young woman has been seen. The barracks occupy the site of a country house, named Greenlaw, that was used as a prison for French soldiers captured in the Napoleonic Wars. She was apparently the daughter of a local man, who had her locked up in her room after having caught her kissing a French soldier. It seems that the prisoners of war were allowed to exercise alone in the adjoining woods and that some of them met local girls there. It is further claimed that the girl's father killed the soldier in question, such was his rage and dislike of Frenchmen. However, there is no record of this murder having taken place. When the girl was given her freedom once more she headed quickly to the woods. When she found out that her lover had been killed she threw herself from the rocks into a deep chasm. This spot is still known as the Lover's Leap, and it is here that the spirit of the girl is most often seen.

Another tale of love results in the ghostly sounds of singing, heard in the district of Mull known as Brolass. Tradition states that there were two sisters of the name MacLean—Elizabeth and Margaret. Their father was the tacksman, or person who leased the ground and sublet it to crofters. The two girls were tall and beautiful, and as a result were visited by many admirers in search of love. Elizabeth was easily pleased and married one of the first men who proposed to her. Margaret had a different temperament altogether and refused all who asked for her hand in marriage. Her parents became annoyed with her stubbornness, but they were never able to persuade her to explain why she turned 'them all down'. Finally her sister Elizabeth managed to squeeze the truth from her, after having sworn to keep the reason a secret.

It seems that Margaret had fallen in love with a man of the name MacDonald, whose clan were then at feud with the MacLeans. Elizabeth was certain that their parents would not allow a marriage to go ahead, and that it would cause serious upset in the family. Margaret told Elizabeth that she and MacDonald planned to elope.

Elizabeth found it impossible to keep her secret and revealed all to her husband. He knew many of Margaret's suitors and arranged with them to prevent the girl eloping with the enemy. As the two lovers headed towards MacDonald's boat one of the conspirators leapt out and stabbed the ill-starred Romeo. Margaret threw herself over his corpse, sobbing inconsolably. She then rose up, and gazing at her dead fiancé, called out, 'The dignity of the Macdonalds.' Turning to her suitors, she cried, 'The conceit of the MacLeans.' She then ran away across the moors. For the next few weeks, she refused to eat or sleep and would ask anyone she met, 'Have you seen my lover?' At length she died, mad with grief and exhaustion.

The song Margaret sang, which is said to be heard echoing through the hills, runs as follows:

My mother's chair is empty, empty and cold,
My father, who loved me, sleeps in death,
My sister, her promise broken, all has told,
I am without kin, without lover, I have only breath.

Sister, may ill befall all that you loved best,
May neither rain nor dew bless the soil you till,
May no child of yours want your arms in rest,
ay your cattle find no food upon the hill.

I am searching the moors and the bens,
All the spots where I courted my dear,
I am searching the mountains and the glens,
But he is not here, not here.

Tradition adds that Margaret's parents died of grief and that her curse resulted in Elizabeth's husband leaving her. She could not afford to look after herself and had to beg from the neighbouring crofts. When she died her ghost remained at Brolass, roaming the district around her former home.

In Fife, located in the cliffs below East Wemyss, are the Wemyss Caves. There were at least nine of these caves, but some are now blocked off for safety reasons. Within them are ancient carvings on the bare rock, the largest such collection in Britain, which date from the Bronze Age. The Court Cave is so-called, because it was once used as a baron-baillie meeting place, where justice was dispensed and wrongdoers put on trial. It is this cave that is said to be haunted by a sixteenth-century female figure: Mary Sibbald. The daughter of a local farmer, she fell in love with a gipsy and ran away from home to travel with him. Mary was accused of stealing and was sentenced to be flogged. The shock of punishment was enough to kill the woman.

Some folk have seen a phantom woman in the nearby ruin of Macduff's Castle, and some say that this too is the spirit of Mary Sibbald. An old lady claims to have seen her looking down from an inaccessible window in the ruins. When a tourist took a photograph of the inside of the cave, it was empty when his flash went off, but when the film was developed a seated woman appears.

In the same county can be found Macduff's Cross, which is located in a triangular field in the low Ochil Hills, a mile south of Newburgh. Sir Walter Scott wrote a poem entitled 'Macduff's Cross' after his visit to the spot, and he regarded the view there as one of the finest in the land. Today the cross is little more than a large boulder, originally the base of a carved cross that has long since disappeared, probably in the Reformation. Tradition states that anyone related to the Macduff Earls of Fife could claim sanctuary here, even if they had committed murder or any other serious crime. All they had to do was donate nine cows and a heifer and wash themselves nine times at the Nine Wells nearby. However, it was said that if kinship with the Fife family could not be proved then the person claiming refuge would be killed instantly. Locals say that the sound of screams deriving from these deaths can still be heard in the locality.

Another place with Bronze Age associations is the Auld Wives' Lifts, located on Craigmaddie Muir to the northeast of Milngavie. The lifts comprise three huge boulders, perched on top of one another. Some say that the stones were placed there by humans, perhaps the Auld Wife of legend: others reckon that they were left in this position by a receding glacier, but in any case the stones have been mentioned in history and legend for centuries. There is a weird ambience near the stones and many visitors describe feeling a shiver run down their spine and the air turning ice cold when they stand in their vicinity. The upper stone has a number of carved faces on it, perhaps wrought by Bronze Age sun-worshippers.

One of the most remote and most attractive beaches in Britain is Sandwood Bay in north-west Sutherland. No road leads to its lonely grandeur; only folk on foot or sailing along the coast can enjoy its beauty. It is now owned by a conservation group, the John Muir Trust. Sandwood boasts a well-known ghost, the spirit of a sailor.

Many folk, considering how remote the bay is, have seen the ghost of the seaman. Many sightings are modem, and all witnesses agree that the man is at least six feet six inches tall and has a beard. He is usually dressed in a long dark overcoat, distinguished by its brass buttons, a faded sailor's cap and old boots. Some have described the style of clothing as eighteenth-century.

The sailor's ghost has been seen all along the mile-long beach, as well as at the only building in the district, Sandwood Cottage, located half a mile inland and overlooking Sandwood Loch. The owner of the Edinburgh house that was haunted by a seaman, mentioned in Chapter 4, is said to have obtained a haunted piece of wood from this cottage.

On the road between Balmaclellan and Corsock, in Galloway, the apparition of a headless piper has been seen. This was witnessed many years ago by a drover who was returning home, having taken cattle to market. A wild storm brewed up and the drover was forced to seek shelter beneath some bushes on Corsock Hill. By the time the foul weather had subsided, darkness had fallen and the drover was in a rush to get home. As he crossed a very remote part of the moor his collie began to whine and kept very close to his master's heels. The drover stopped for a minute to see if he could find out what was bothering the dog. From the glen he could hear the sound of bagpipes growing ever louder, and frightening the dog even more. Suddenly a flash of blue light appeared in front of the drover and within its midst he could see a figure playing the pipes, moving to and fro. The piper walked towards the drover, who could now see that the body had no head and was so thin that it was virtually see-through. There was another flash of light, followed by a loud clap of thunder that threw the drover to the ground. When the vision had passed, the drover rushed to the farm cottage where he was to spend the night. He relayed his experience to the old farmer, who replied. 'Ay, ay, lad, ye ha'e seen the ghost o'the piper who was murdered on his way frae Patiesthorn. I ha'e had the same fearsome experience myself, though it's mair than saxty years syne.'

The White Lady of Tarras haunts the moors around Langholm in Dumfriesshire. The Tarras Water drains the hills east of the town, flowing past Tarras Lodge. Some time in the nineteenth century an agricultural worker named John Graham was walking in the vicinity one evening. He became aware of someone following him, and saw that it was a lady dressed completely in white. His step became longer and quicker and soon he arrived at a blacksmith's shop. In a state of shock he told the smith what he had seen. The smith explained that he had witnessed a well-known local ghost, the White Lady.

The blacksmith went on to explain the story behind the haunting. Years ago a cottager named Archie Brown and his wife were visited by a woman late one night. From her dress they could tell that she came from a well-off family. She had been travelling across the county and gradually became exhausted: could she thus spend the night with the Browns? Next morning the lady rewarded the family with money taken from a purse that Archie spotted was full of gold coins. He volunteered to go with the woman part of her way, but on the moors of Tarras he murdered her and stole her gold and jewellery. Her spirit returned to haunt him, and has also been seen by many others.

Staying in the south of Scotland we find the tale of the Rerrick poltergeist. This well-known haunting achieved great fame when the happenings occurred. The local minister details everything in a pamphlet entitled 'A True Relation of an Apparition, Expressions and Actings of a Spirit which infested the House of Andrew Mackie, in Ring-Croft of Stocking, in the Paroch of Rerrick in the Stewartry of Kirkcudbright in Scotland, 1695, by Mr Alexander Telfair, Minister of that Paroch and Attested by Many Other Persons, who were also Eye and Ear Witnesses.' It was also recorded in an early edition of the *Encyclopaedia Britannica*.

At first the Mackies found that their cattle kept being loosened overnight, despite having been tied up in the byre. No matter how well Andrew fastened the knots they were always undone the next morning. At length he decided to leave the cattle loose, but awoke the next day to find that one cow was tied up at the back of the cottage, its feet bound very tightly. No explanation for this could be worked out by Andrew Mackie.

At the beginning of March that year small pebbles began to launch themselves around the inside of the house. Where they had come from no one knew. One day the children arrived home and saw what they thought was a body seated by the kitchen range. When they went to look close they discovered that there was now only a blanket on a chair. As the days passed, the stones being thrown in the house got bigger, and things began to disappear. The hooks used to hold up the pots and pans vanished. The whole house was searched for them without success. Four days later they were found in the loft, which had already been checked more than once.

After the service next Sunday Andrew Mackie told the minister about the happenings and appealed to him for help. The Revd Alexander Telfair called on the Tuesday, when he said a number of prayers. He witnessed a few small stones being thrown about, but nothing as serious as the Mackies had experienced. At a later date he, the laird and some others spent part of the night at the cottage and again saw stones moving about. As the minister prayed he felt a hand on his arm and on opening his eyes spotted a white arm and hand that soon vanished. Another witness saw a young boy of around fourteen years old.

The occurrences gradually intensified, the family and visitors being beaten by sticks and showered with stones. A group of ministers visited but were abused in the same way, Revd Andrew Ewart being injured and his wig being pulled off! Stones were thrown about the house and a burning peat landed amongst folk at prayer.

Mrs Mackie became aware that the stone step at the front door had become loose and shook when stood on. When she lifted it she found bones and fresh-looking blood. She ran to the laird's house for help and on returning they found the house in a bigger turmoil than usual, with burning peats, hot stones and fireballs flying about. A large staff had been forced through the wall next to the children's bed. When the bones were removed from below the step the disturbances ceased.

Five ministers arrived at the cottage with the Revd Telfair, where they were to fast and pray. The stones began flying around the house as soon as the prayers started, and the person reciting them seemed to suffer the beatings worst of all. The spirit even began to say 'Take you that' as it hit them, and 'Wheesht' as prayers were being said. For a number of days the house was set on fire repeatedly; no sooner had the men managed to douse the flames than another fire blew up. This continued for some time, and on one occasion the end of the house was pulled down. A large fire seems finally to have forced the folk to stay in the byre. A further fire burned down the sheep shed. The sheep were saved, and from that time the happenings unaccountably ceased and never returned.

Another poltergeist disrupted a family living at Sunipol Farm on the island of Mull. This is located at Mornish, the north-west corner of the island. A man named Campbell emigrated to Australia, where he lived a life of crime, robbing houses and shops. He later returned to Mull, setting up home with his family at Sunipol. On many occasions stones from the shore would inexplicably throw themselves at his home, and other objects were noted flying around the house. There were even reports of spectral Australian aborigines. Campbell's two sisters at one time hired two men with guns to shoot the spirits that appeared there, but it is said that no one but the Campbells could see or hear them. The house is again occupied by a Campbell, but the present proprietor has not seen any signs of ghosts or poltergeists.

On the road through Nithsdale, south of Sanquhar in Dumfriesshire, can be found the home of another lady dressed in white. This ghost, which appears near to Dalpeddar

Farm, is known as 'Lady Hebron'. She is often seen carrying a child, which is sometimes heard screaming. Many years ago Hebron inherited her father's property and was married. However, her husband died soon after the birth of their son. An uncle who had his eyes on the property, is said to have murdered Hebron and her son, for they were never seen alive again. Years late the skeleton of a woman and child were found in the locality, the woman's skull rent by an axe or other sharp implement.

In the latter half of the nineteenth century William Wilson was travelling between Qrumlanrig and Sanquhar. He tells what he saw:

> Judge of my astonishment when, near to the noted tree, and right in the middle of the road and coming towards me, I saw a tall lady dressed all in white. My first impression was anything but pleasant, for I had long known the uncanny tale told of the spot. However, I thought, if spirit it is, it will be useless trying to evade it. I accordingly determined to face it, taking a firmer grip of the oak staff I carried. Her ladyship came slowly on, and as we passed each other I observed that 'it was a nice, calm night'. Her ghostship, however, made no answer. Whether or not this was Lady Hebron's ghost or not I never could learn. At all events she did not interfere with me. When she had passed I turned round and watched her until she was out of sight.

At Conon Ferry in Ross and Cromarty the tale of Fairburn's Ghost lives on. The ferryman was just finishing his day's work, transporting folk back and forth across the River Conon and was tying up his boat for the night. Suddenly he became aware of a man watching him, who asked to be taken across the river. Recognizing him as the MacKenzie laird of Fairburn Tower, the ferryman reluctantly agreed. On the other side the laird asked the ferryman to accompany him on his journey as it was now quite late. This request was not typical of the laird, but the ferryman agreed to walk part of the way with him. It was a wild night, and storms were blowing across the mountains of Ross. A few streaks of lightning lit up the sky, allowing the ferryman a closer look at Fairburn. He was startled to discover that it was a corpse he was accompanying. It was later discovered that MacKenzie of Fairburn had died suddenly a few hours beforehand.

The burgh of Dornoch in Sutherland has a large slab of whinstone, known as the Witch's Stone, which is located in a garden on the edge of a golf course. This marks the spot where in 1722 Janet Home was burned at the stake for practising witchcraft. It was claimed that she had changed her own daughter into a pony and had her shod by the devil. As a result she was tarred, feathered and roasted to death. She is thought to be the last witch to have been burned in Scotland. Local tradition has it that on clear autumn nights, when the moon is waning, her ghost can be seen in the vicinity.

Another spirit said to consort with the devil makes irregular appearances at the Loch of Skene in Aberdeenshire. This ghost is most often seen on Hogmanay (New Year's Eve) and consists of a horse-drawn carriage, ridden by the local laird, Alexander Skene of that Ilk (1680–1724), who owned Skene House. The horses tend to be black in colour, and some folk claim that they are headless. Skene was rumoured in the district to be a wizard, and many tales linking him with the underworld went the rounds. He is said to have journeyed to Italy where he studied the black arts for seven years and that he was often accompanied on his travels by a black crow and other living symbols of the devil. It was also claimed that he fed to his familiars unbaptized children, which he dug up in the kirkyard, and that his body cast no shadows, even in strong sunlight. Tales of the phantom coach and horses originated shortly after his death.

To the south of Aviemore in Inverness-shire is the very attractive Loch Alvie, another haunted loch. An old tradition in the area has it that the loch is haunted by a ghostly washer-woman. This spectre, known in Gaelic custom as a 'Bean-nigheadaireachd', appears to those who are about to die. I can only suggest that those who read this book, and who wish to witness a ghost or haunting of their own, choose a different spot for seeking them out than Loch Alvie.

BIBLIOGRAPHY

Ansdell, Ian, *Strange Tales of Old Edinburgh*. Lang Syne, 1975.
Bailey, Helen, *My Love Affair with Borthwick Castle*. Book Guild, 1988.
Boucher, Robert, *The Kingdom of Fife: Its Ballads and Legends*. Dundee, 1899.
Brookesworth, Peter (ed.), *Great Hauntings*. Orbis Publishing, 1984.
Brooks, John, *The Good Ghost Guide*. Jarrold Publishing, 1994.
Campbell, Margaret, *Ghosts, Massacres, and Horror Stories of Scotland's Castles*. Lang Syne, n.d.
Chambers, Robert, *Traditions of Edinburgh*. Chambers, 1823.
Cohen, Daniel, *Encyclopedia of Ghosts*. Michael O'Mara Books, 1984
Coxe, Antony D. Hippisley, *Haunted Britain*. Hutchinson 1973.
Dick, Charles Hill, *Highways and Byways in Galloway and Carrick*. Macmillan, 1916.
Folklore, Myths and Legends of Britain. Reader's Digest, 1973.
Forman, Joan, *Haunted Royal Homes*. Harrap, 1987
Frew, Christine, *Ghost Stories from the Clyde Valley*. Clyde Valley Tourist Board, n.d.
Goodrich-Freer, A., and Bute, John, Marquess of, *The Alleged Haunting of B[allechin] House. 1899.*
Graham, Angus, *Skipness: Memoirs of a Highland Estate*. Canongate, 1993.
Gray, Affleck, *The Big Grey Man of Ben MacDhui*. Impulse Books, 1970.
—*Legends of the Cairngorms*. Mainstream, 1987.
Green, Andrew, *Haunted Houses*. Shire Publications, 1975.
Halifax, Lord, *Lord Halifax's Ghost Book. 1936.*
Hannan, Thomas, *Famous Scottish Houses*. A & C Black, 1928.
Hapgood, Sarah, *500 British Ghosts and Hauntings*. Foulsham, 1993.
—*The World's Great Ghost and Poltergeist Stories*. Foulsham, 1994.
Harper, Charles G., *Haunted Houses*. Chapman & Hall, 1907.
Herbert, William Barry, *Railway Ghosts and Phantoms*. David & Charles, 1989.
Ingram, John H., *The Haunted Homes and Family Traditions of Great Britain*. Reeves & Turner, 1905.
Lamont-Brown, Raymond, *The Life and Times of St Andrews*. John Donald, 1989.
Linskill, William T., *St Andrews Ghost Stories*.
MacGregor, Alasdair Alpin, *The Ghost Book*. Robert Hale, 1955.
—*Phantom Footsteps*, Robert Hale, 1959.
McKerracher, Archie C., *Perthshire in History and Legend*. John Donald, 1988.
MacPhail, Colin and Mitchell, Robin, *Adam Lyal's Witchery Tales*. The Cadies, 1988.
Marshall, Francis, *Living With Spirits*. Harlequin Books, 1993.
Mead, Robin, *Weekend Haunts*. Impact Books, 1994.

O'Donnell, Elliott, *Casebook of Ghosts* (edited by Harry Ludlum). W. Foulsham, 1969.
—*Scottish Ghost Stories.* Jarrold Publishing, 1975.
Pease, Howard, *Border Ghost Stories.* Erskine MacDonald, 1919.
Randles, Jenny, and Hough, Peter, *Strange But True?* LWT Productions, 1994.
Robertson, Ronald Macdonald, *Selected Highland Folktales.* Oliver & Boyd, 1961.
Robson, Alan, *Nightmare on Your Street.* Virgin Books, 1993.
Swire, Otta F., *The Inner Hebrides and their Legends.* Collins, 1964.
Temperley, Alan, *Tales of the North Coast.* Research Publishing Company, 1977.
—*Tales of Galloway,* Skilton & Shaw, 1979.
Thomson, Francis, *Ghosts, Spirits and Spectres of Scotland.* Impulse Books, 1973.
—*The Supernatural Highlands.* Robert Hale, 1976.
Tirtoprodjo, Irene, *Ghosts of Tweeddale,* n.d.
Tranter, Nigel, *The Fortified House in Scotland* (5 vols), Oliver & Boyd, 1962.
—*Nigel Tranter's Scotland,* Richard Drew, 1981.
Turnbull, Michael T.R.B., *Edinburgh Characters.* St Andrew Press, 1992.
Underwood, Peter, *Gazetteer of British Ghosts.* Souvenir Press, 1971.
—*Gazetteer of Scottish and Irish Ghosts.* Souvenir Press, 1973.
—*This Haunted Isle.* Harrap,1984
—*The Ghosthunter's Almanac.* Eric Dobby, 1993.
—*Nights in Haunted Houses.* Headline, 1994.
Warner, Gerald, *Tales of the Scottish Highlands.* Shepheard Walwyn, 1982.
Whitaker, Terence, *Scotland's Ghosts and Apparitions.* Robert Hale, 1991.
Williams, Guy, *A Guide to the Magical Places of England, Wales and Scotland,* Constable, 1987.
Wilson, Alan J., Brogan, Des, and McGrail, Frank, *Ghostly Tales and Sinister Stories of Old Edinburgh.* Mainstream, 1991.
Wilson, John Mackay, *Tales of the Borders. 1834.*
Wilson, William, *Folk Lore and Genealogies of Uppermost Nithsdale.* Robert Mann, 1904.

In the course of research, the author has also referred to numerous local guidebooks as well as reports and articles that have appeared in various newspapers, magazines, tourist brochures and hotel advertisements over the years. He has listened to accounts related to him in person by folk who either live in haunted buildings, or else have witnessed ghosts in some form or other. The main publications referred to include the *Daily Record*, [Glasgow] *Herald*, *Scotland on Sunday*, *Scots Magazine*, *Scottish Field*, *Scottish Memories*, *Sunday Post*, *The Field*, *Fortean Tim*es and many other provincial newspapers and magazines.

INDEX